Cambridge Elements

Elements in American Politics
edited by
Frances E. Lee
Princeton University

MONEY, PARTISANSHIP AND POWER IN LOCAL POLITICS

Robert G. Boatright
Clark University
Lane Cuthbert
University of Massachusetts
Adam Eichen
University of Massachusetts
Raymond J. La Raja
University of Massachusetts
Meredith Rolfe
University of Massachusetts

Shaftesbury Road, Cambridge CB2 8EA, United Kingdom

One Liberty Plaza, 20th Floor, New York, NY 10006, USA

477 Williamstown Road, Port Melbourne, VIC 3207, Australia

314–321, 3rd Floor, Plot 3, Splendor Forum, Jasola District Centre, New Delhi – 110025, India

103 Penang Road, #05–06/07, Visioncrest Commercial, Singapore 238467

Cambridge University Press is part of Cambridge University Press & Assessment, a department of the University of Cambridge.

We share the University's mission to contribute to society through the pursuit of education, learning and research at the highest international levels of excellence.

www.cambridge.org
Information on this title: www.cambridge.org/9781009613736

DOI: 10.1017/9781009613743

© Robert G. Boatright, Lane Cuthbert, Adam Eichen, Raymond J. La Raja, and Meredith Rolfe 2025

This publication is in copyright. Subject to statutory exception and to the provisions of relevant collective licensing agreements, no reproduction of any part may take place without the written permission of Cambridge University Press & Assessment.

When citing this work, please include a reference to the DOI 10.1017/9781009613743

First published 2025

A catalogue record for this publication is available from the British Library

ISBN 978-1-009-61371-2 Hardback
ISBN 978-1-009-61373-6 Paperback
ISSN 2515-1606 (online)
ISSN 2515-1592 (print)

Additional resources for this publication at http://www.Cambridge.org/Boatright

Cambridge University Press & Assessment has no responsibility for the persistence or accuracy of URLs for external or third-party internet websites referred to in this publication and does not guarantee that any content on such websites is, or will remain, accurate or appropriate.

For EU product safety concerns, contact us at Calle de José Abascal, 56, 1°, 28003 Madrid, Spain, or email eugpsr@cambridge.org

Money, Partisanship and Power in Local Politics

Elements in American Politics

DOI: 10.1017/9781009613743
First published online: November 2025

Robert G. Boatright
Clark University

Lane Cuthbert
University of Massachusetts

Adam Eichen
University of Massachusetts

Raymond J. La Raja
University of Massachusetts

Meredith Rolfe
University of Massachusetts

Author for correspondence: Robert Boatright, rboatright@clarku.edu

Abstract: This Element presents an analysis of campaign finance in city council elections in four midsize Massachusetts cities. It shows that while money does not determine local election outcomes it plays a gatekeeping role – especially for nonincumbents. Moreover, this money comes from a very unrepresentative segment of the electorate. Although elections in these cities are nonpartisan, individual donors and interest groups are sorted into networks that function like political parties. The Element also shows that donors tend to be substantially more liberal than city residents. This can lead cities to adopt policies that are at odds with the views and needs of cities' less-wealthy inhabitants, including racial minorities. Despite low financial stakes relative to national races, campaign finance in midsize city elections reflects and reinforces broader patterns of political inequality. The result is a campaign finance system that disadvantages city residents who lack the cues that exist in other elections.

Keywords: Urban Politics, Municipal Elections, City Council, Campaign Finance, Political Parties, Interest Groups, Labor Unions

© Robert G. Boatright, Lane Cuthbert, Adam Eichen, Raymond J. La Raja, Meredith Rolfe 2025

ISBNs: 9781009613712 (HB), 9781009613736 (PB), 9781009613743 (OC)
ISSNs: 2515-1606 (online), 2515-1592 (print)

Contents

	Introduction	1
1	Money and Elections in Midsize Cities	6
2	Four Midsize Massachusetts Cities	16
3	The Candidates	21
4	Donors	40
5	Parties	53
6	Interest Groups	72
7	Conclusions and Implications	84
	Bibliography	91

Online Appendix available at http://www.Cambridge.org/Boatright

Introduction

On May 28, 2024, the Worcester, Massachusetts City Council chamber was packed. Residents had come to comment on the how the addition of protected bike lanes to Mill Street, a major city thoroughfare, had affected their lives. Safety experts had endorsed the change, and the council had previously supported it unanimously. But a fatal car crash, amplified by a Facebook group organized by the campaign manager of a losing candidate, had triggered a political firestorm (McNamara 2024).

At the hearing, the room fractured along invisible lines. Well-dressed bike lane advocates from a cycling and environmental nonprofit, Walk Bike Worcester, cited traffic data and urban planning research. Opponents, many of them older and working class, told stories of confusion and danger. One woman implored the council not to make Worcester into "another Cambridge." Under mounting pressure, two councilors reversed their votes. The redesign narrowly survived, but future projects were shelved (Bass 2024). The final vote pitted the councilors generally regarded as the most progressive against those with reputations for being more conservative.

Forty miles east, the city of Cambridge also had experienced battles over bicycle safety, but the dominant issue in its recent elections has been housing. Over the past several elections, three local organizations funded by wealthy donors, A Better Cambridge, the Cambridge Residents Alliance, and the Cambridge Citizens Coalition, have offered housing and environmental proposals, endorsed candidate slates, and educated citizens about the city's voting laws. A fourth organization, the Cambridge Bicycle Safety Independent Expenditure PAC, also slated candidates, and three other groups, including the Democratic Socialists of America and Our Revolution (an organization with ties to Vermont Senator Bernie Sanders) also made endorsements.

Two other Massachusetts cities, Lowell and Springfield, have also experienced some bitter election campaigns. In Lowell, conflict over where to build a new high school led to the formation of a group entitled Building a Stronger Commonwealth Independent Expenditure PAC. This group, funded by labor unions and by donors who did not live in Lowell, distributed yard signs late in the campaign calling some council members "puppets" and "clowns" and raising allegations of financial and sexual improprieties (Mills 2019). And in Springfield, city council candidates bickered throughout the 2010s and early 2020s over whether to suspend the city's $90 trash fee for residents. They alternately framed the trash fee as an unjustified tax on citizens, a financially prudent means of balancing the city budget, or a barrier to more environmentally responsible ways of reducing waste (Snowden 2023).

At first glance, these conflicts appear to have little in common. They do not necessarily resemble the ideological fault lines that determine many votes in the United States Congress, or in American state legislatures. Yet despite the fact that these cities, like many American municipalities, have nonpartisan elections, the dynamics were strikingly similar. In each city, progressive reforms championed by well-educated elites met resistance from voters who felt left out. The money for and against reform came not from a broad base, but from a small set of politically connected donors. Political competition unfolded not through formal parties, but through networks, slates, and social media campaigns – and, we suspect, most citizens of these cities had little knowledge that these networks even existed. These networks pose a paradox: although urban elections appear to be grassroots affairs where voters have many opportunities to meet their elected officials, these campaigns tend to be financed by a narrow, unrepresentative slice of the public. Policy outcomes, in turn, often reflect the priorities of donors, not citizens.

This Element is a study of the ways in which money, partisanship, and power shaped elections in midsize American cities. As we shall demonstrate, the dynamics we associate with national politics – such as polarization, elite influence, and ideological sorting – are very much alive at the local level. The mechanisms may be more subtle than at the national level, but the stakes are no less consequential.

In this Element we use data about candidate fundraising and donor networks to trace the structure of politics in these midsize cities. In doing this, we exploit a novel way to examine politics in places where good data are often limited and therefore analysis remains underdeveloped. We make five significant contributions to the study of local elections:

1. *Candidates:* We investigate fundraising by council and mayoral candidates, showing that money does matter in these elections, but that it matters far more for efforts to get into office than it does for those who are already there. More so than in other types of elections, incumbents have an advantage, making it difficult for citizens to bring about changes in their representation. Our findings suggest that candidates do not need to raise significant sums. Local elections are often uncontested and low turnout affairs, where political elites do not attempt to mobilize voters beyond those who already pay some attention to politics.

Candidates running for at-large seats or for mayor must raise and spend more to communicate over a larger area. We find (but cannot demonstrate strongly with our case studies) that candidates running in a strong mayoral system raise more money because the stakes appear higher for this office.

2. *Donors:* We explore the characteristics of donors, showing that donors, even at the grassroots level of municipal elections, are highly unrepresentative of their cities' populations. They are more likely to be white, and they tend to be older, wealthier, and, on average, substantially more ideological in their political views. Donors are embedded in elite political networks with other donors, and to the degree candidates get the support of these distinctive networks, they tend to perform better in the election. In short, there are significant inequalities in who gives and who participates in politics.

3. *Parties:* We show through our analysis of campaign money that despite an electoral system that is ostensibly nonpartisan, three of the four cities in fact have organized factions that function like political parties. We argue that these factions may often be based in existing ideological, socioeconomic, and racial cleavages, but that the existence of these cleavages does not solely determine the development of factional politics at the local level. In other words, there is factional politics but it is less structured at the local level than at higher levels of government.

4. *Interest Groups:* We show that interest groups give mostly to build relationships and highlight support for particular candidates, but the total amount donated by political action committees (PACs) is generally small compared to the total donations made by individuals. However, some interest groups weigh in occasionally with independent spending to put their stamp on a policy issue and set the campaign agenda. This is an electoral tactic that has become prominent in elections for higher offices, and it has trickled into local elections.

5. *Election Systems:* Institutional and electoral contexts matter. While our design does not demonstrate causal linkages, we find that cities with different electoral systems (single transferable vote versus plurality systems, or at-large versus district systems) appear to exhibit distinct patterns of fundraising and donor behavior.

Theories of local governance in the U.S. have traditionally emphasized how fragmented authority, institutional design, and political economy shape urban power. Postwar research focused on who governs American cities, how power is structured and exercised, and why cities make the decisions they do. Some early authors highlighted the dominance of business elites behind the scenes (Hunter 1953), while others offered a more pluralist interpretation, suggesting that political power was distributed across competing groups with influence over different domains (Dahl 1961). Building on critiques of pluralism, scholars introduced a second dimension of power – how elites shape agendas by preventing certain issues from surfacing (Bachrach and Baratz 1962). Later structuralist arguments emphasized that cities prioritize economic growth over redistribution due to interjurisdictional competition for capital (Peterson 1981).

These ideas were revised by urban regime theory, which argues that cities are governed through informal but durable coalitions that combine political legitimacy with organizational and economic resources (Stone 1989). Over time, scholars expanded this framework to identify different types of regimes, from pro-growth alliances to community-based partnerships (Imbroscio 1997; Mossberger and Stoker 2001). Critics, however, have questioned the framework's ongoing relevance and business-centric assumptions, especially in smaller or fragmented cities. This has led to alternative perspectives such as network governance, which emphasize decentralized, issue-specific coalitions (Stone 2005) and the institutional capacity needed to address complex local problems (Clarke 1998). Related research highlights how informal rules and intergovernmental networks help solve collective action dilemmas (Feiock 2009).

More recent work focuses on how electoral institutions and structural inequalities shape local participation and representation. Political monopolies can make local government less responsive to public preferences, while district design influences representational equity (Trounstine 2008; Trounstine and Valdini 2008). The absence of partisan cues weakens voters' ability to select ideologically aligned candidates (Schaffner, Streb, and Wright 2001). In low-salience elections, interest groups such as unions and developers can wield disproportionate influence (Anzia 2022). Civic inequality also matters: engagement is skewed toward older, wealthier, and whiter residents (Schiff 2022), and community networks play dual roles in either supporting or constraining political participation (Benjamin 2017). Declining local journalism further erodes civic knowledge and accountability (Darr, Hitt, and Dunway 2021). Together, these studies suggest that political inequality is reinforced through institutional design, elite mobilization, and information gaps.

Finally, a growing body of research explores the role of ideology and partisanship in shaping local governance. Although local elections often favor affluent, organized constituencies (Oliver, Ha, and Callen 2012), policies frequently align with the ideological leanings of residents (Tausanovitch and Warshaw 2014, 2021). However, these outcomes often fail to represent lower-income and nonwhite voters due to low engagement and limited information (Schaffner, Rhodes, and La Raja 2020). The increasing nationalization of local politics further amplifies this trend, as voters apply national partisan identities even in nonpartisan contests (Hopkins 2018). Partisan control of city hall has concrete consequences for outcomes such as fiscal policy and housing policy (de Benedictis-Kessner and Warshaw 2016; de Benedictis-Kessner, Jones, and Warshaw 2025), and recent work also shows how municipal campaign contributions affect responsiveness to development interests (Gaudette and de Benedictis-Kessner, 2024, working paper). This literature underscores that local political outcomes emerge not only from formal institutions but also from patterns of ideological polarization, elite donor activity, and structural inequality.

The findings from *Money, Partisanship, and Power in Local Politics* extend this body of research by showing how campaign finance and informal partisan alignments shape political competition and representation in midsize cities. While much prior work emphasizes either elite coalitions or voter-level dynamics, this study bridges the two by examining the donor networks, ideological factions, and informal organizations that operate in the absence of strong local party infrastructure. In cities such as Worcester, Lowell, Springfield, and Cambridge, political actors leverage money to create influence ecosystems that substitute for traditional parties, shaping candidate emergence, electoral competition, and policy agendas. The Element highlights how ideologically extreme donors – often white, older, and affluent – fill the void left by declining civic infrastructure and low public engagement, particularly in under-institutionalized electoral environments. This contributes a novel lens to the study of local governance: one that centers money not just as a resource, but as an organizing force in urban political life. By tracing how campaign finance flows through local factions and reinforces inequalities in voice and representation, the Element helps explain why local democracy remains distorted even in formally open systems. It offers a grounded account of how power operates through informal political structures and how financial asymmetries interact with institutional weakness to produce persistent inequities in urban policymaking.

We are able to conduct this analysis because we have merged two sources of data. First, since 2005 Massachusetts has required mayoral and city council candidates in all cities with populations over 100,000 residents to report all of their campaign receipts and expenditures to the state.

This enables us to compile full donor lists of identical quality for multiple cities over an extended time period. Second, we were able to merge these records with the voter database compiled by Catalist LLC. Catalist is a national firm that collects and processes voter data and its primary customer base consists of (progressive) campaigns. Catalist's dataset consists of voter files that it obtains from the states, which are checked for accuracy and standardized. Catalist then supplements these voter lists with racial, demographic, and political data for each voter that it obtains or derives from a variety of sources, such as the Census, select commercial sources (for information on income, wealth, and homeownership), and proprietary models that are developed in-house to predict values (for partisanship, ideology, and race/ethnicity). A variety of studies comparing Catalist results to survey data have found these predictive models to be highly accurate.[1] In our analysis we matched Catalist data on attributes such as the race, ethnicity, age, length of residence, income, and ideology (as defined by Catalist's "ideology plus" model) of each donor in these cities' elections. This method enables us to develop a far more detailed understanding of who these donors are than is possible through surveys or any other means of study.

Section 1 of this Element explains why it is important to look at midsize cities. Section 2 describes the four cities we have chosen to study and offers details on our method of study. Section 3 discusses patterns in candidate fundraising across these four cities, Section 4 describes the characteristics of donors, Section 5 identifies and describes the role of parties and party-like organizations, and Section 6 discusses the role of other organized groups and their relationship to local factional groups. Section 7 discusses the lessons we might take from this study for the study of urban politics, political inequality, and campaign finance.

1 Money and Elections in Midsize Cities

The financing of American elections at the federal and state levels is well documented, and many scholars who study these elections conclude that money is an essential component of elections. It might strike some readers as nice to conclude that local elections are not driven by money, but it is hard to know whether this is the case. Studies of voter turnout in city elections generally conclude that because turnout is so low, the voices of older and wealthier citizens tend to be amplified. Are these people also financing local campaigns? If one wishes to learn about the financing of these

---

[1] For a recent summary of this literature, see Kim and Fraga 2022.

campaigns, one is often at the mercy of city clerks or a maze of local and state laws. To make matters more complicated, existing research on local elections has to date focused largely on a small number of large American cities. As we discuss in greater detail below, scholars have analyzed campaign finance and campaign finance laws in large cities such as New York, Chicago, and Los Angeles, and some recent studies have analyzed elections in cities such as Seattle, where innovative new ideas about campaign finance have been implemented. Yet most Americans do not reside in the nation's largest cities, and we have no way of knowing from these studies whether findings about elections in large cities are applicable to smaller cities.

One goal of this project is to fill this gap. We analyze patterns in campaign finance over an eighteen-year period in four midsize cities. Midsize cities – those cities with populations between 75,000 and 500,000 – are home to approximately twenty percent of the U.S. population. These cities are also growing at a more rapid pace than the nation's largest cities (Homann 2015; Raetz 2021). Running for office is less costly in such places than in larger cities, innovations in election financing can face fewer obstacles, and it can be easier to conduct comparative studies than is the case for larger cities. There is also a public policy benefit to understanding how the financing of elections in midsize cities differs from the financing of campaigns in other parts of the country. Midsize cities have different characteristics than larger metropolitan areas, at least in the Eastern United States, where we focus our work. According to the Federal Reserve Bank's program on midsize cities, they are more likely than larger cities to attract immigrants, they face distinctive economic challenges, and their population is younger on average than that of larger cities (Rosengren 2012). Yet the Federal Reserve Bank's urban economists also argue that these cities are often left out of regional political and economic development plans.

Apart from filling a gap in the literature and addressing needs specific to midsize cities, research on campaign finance in smaller cities can also help us to understand how new ideas for reform have fared. At a moment when federal campaign finance reform efforts seem paralyzed, some reform advocates have sought to understand the consequences at the state and local levels of public financing laws, alternative voting schemes such as ranked choice voting (RCV), or single transferable vote (STV) and other such reforms.[2] Given their smaller size, it is easier to change election laws

---

[2] STV, also known as proportional ranked-choice voting, is a method of choosing multiple candidates for a legislative body by using a single ranked-choice ballot. We use the term

at the local level than at the state and federal levels, and such changes can help us to understand how these reforms can scale up.

This Element draws on data we have collected for all contributions to city council candidates in four midsize cities in Massachusetts – Worcester, Springfield, Lowell, and Cambridge – over nine election cycles from 2005 to 2021. Comparing campaign finance data across these four cities can help us to understand how city characteristics such as population size, electoral system, income levels and growth, or media market overlap have on the costs of campaigns and the sources of contributions. One of these four midsize cities (Cambridge) has used STV in its elections since 1941, and two of these cities switched from at-large elections to district elections during this time period. We cannot prove that these cities are representative of all midsize cities – and in the obvious case of geography, of course, they are not – but throughout, we argue that many of our findings can be generalized to other, similar cities.

1.1 What We Know about Municipal Campaign Finance

While researchers have made great strides in gathering data on municipal election outcomes (e.g., de Benedictis-Kessner et al. 2023), there are still few comparative studies of municipal campaign finance. There is no federal standard for the reporting of municipal campaign finance data, so reporting varies according to state regulations. Some cities or states provide municipal data in a downloadable or searchable format, while others make candidate contribution records available as large pdf documents or allow interested researchers to peruse printed forms at city hall. Nearly all states set thresholds for campaign finance reporting according to city size.

It is also difficult to conduct comparisons between cities because of variations in government structure, in whether elections are partisan, or in the size of cities or council districts. This stands in contrast to state and federal elections, where the offices and election laws are sufficiently comparable that one can make broad statements about, for instance, the cost of winning a congressional seat and a state legislative seat. Many existing studies of municipal campaign finance are thus limited to studies of particular large cities, such as New York, Chicago, or Los Angeles (see below for citations). The most comprehensive study of municipal campaign finance, by Adams (2010, 2011), considers the financing of elections in twelve cities,

---

STV here to distinguish it from single-candidate RCV, which is used in some states to choose individual legislators or statewide officials.

ranging in size from a population of 260,000 (Lexington, Kentucky) to 8,000,000 (New York). One could certainly use some of these studies to make general claims about the financing of elections in large cities, but it remains possibly that elections in smaller cities might not share these traits.

There are three major ways in which other scholars have approached the study of municipal campaign finance.

1.1.1 Comparing Municipal Campaign Finance to State and Federal Campaign Finance

First, studies of municipal campaign finance can be compared to the much more developed literature on state and federal campaign finance. Studies of this sort tend to focus on the candidates – which candidates tend to be most successful at raising money, and how might an aspiring candidate for office develop a fundraising strategy? Research on congressional candidates' fundraising practices has shown that incumbents tend to substantially outraise their opponents and that they do so in part because of their ability to attract contributions from business-oriented PACs or other access-seeking donors (Fouirnaies and Hall 2014). Particularly ideological candidates often excel at raising small contributions or contributions from partisan individual donors who reside outside of the candidates' state or district (Johnson 2010). Similarly, research on congressional campaign contributors has consistently shown that individual contributors are disproportionately wealthy, white, and male (Francia, Green, Herrnson, Powell, and Wilcox 2003, 30; Heerwig 2016). Numerous studies of congressional candidates and donors, as well as studies of candidates and donors in presidential elections (Magleby, Goodliffe, and Olson 2018), gubernatorial elections (Jensen and Beyle 2003), and state legislative elections (Powell 2012) have documented similar patterns.

To date, candidate studies have been the most common approaches to municipal campaign finance, in part because it is easy to acquire contribution data for at least some cities and to make inferences based on the sources of funds for candidates. One might expect local election candidates to share the traits noted earlier for state and federal candidates. However, there is also some reason to expect differences at the local level due to differences in elections, as documented earlier, and due to the different ways local politicians might use money. Campaign contributions are a matter of supply and demand – and the demand of politicians for contributions may be lower when politicians have less need for money or fewer ways to spend that money. In his 2010 book, Adams argues that incumbent city officeholders tend to enjoy an advantage comparable to that of U.S. representatives, that the contributor pool in local elections is even wealthier than that of congressional elections, and that business interests tend to dominate local elections. Precisely because so few citizens are paying attention and because, in most cities, voters lack obvious cues such as partisanship, candidates who can easily raise a threshold amount of money from the local business community are able to win local office and then can easily stay there. Lieske (1989) reaches similar conclusions about campaign contributions in his study of Cincinnati elections, arguing that there is a logarithmic relationship between vote share and candidate receipts.

Studies specific to particular cities, however, have qualified some of these findings. Krebs (1998) showed that in Chicago aldermanic elections, money plays less of a role in determining the vote share for incumbents than it does for open seat candidates and challengers; he argues that incumbents can frequently develop personal ties with voters that make campaign spending unnecessary. Studies of Chicago elections also draw attention to the role of corporate or labor interests in these elections – while there is an overall bias toward wealthier contributors and corporate interests, the appearance of contentious issues on the council agenda can provoke substantial labor spending from time to time and can produce some elections where contribution patterns differ sharply from those preceding or following them (Hogan and Simpson 2001; Krebs and Pelissero 2001; Hennessy 2013). Research by Krebs (2004) comparing Chicago and Los Angeles also supports these claims.

In their comparison of campaign finance in cities in Ontario, Kushner, Siegel, and Stanwick (1997) show that campaign finance is more closely correlated with candidate success in larger cities than in smaller ones. They argue that the cost of paid voter contact, such as radio and television advertising, direct mail, and yard signs, become more important as the size of the constituency increases; although large cities can in theory have small council districts, for the most part constituency size also increases with city size. Fleischman and Stein (1998) compare contributions in Atlanta and St. Louis. They contend that, in contrast to the U.S. Congress, one's status within a local government – for example, whether one holds a leadership position or committee chair within the council – has no relationship to fundraising ability. Arrington and Ingalls (1984) contend in their study of elections in Charlotte, North Carolina that there are discrepancies in the contribution strategies of African American and white donors – African American donors concentrate their donations narrowly on African

American candidates while white donors give more diffusely to whites and Blacks. As a result, they argue, a majority white city council may still have well-financed minority candidates.

Oliver, Ha, and Callan (2012, 112) paint a more nuanced picture of the relationship between city size and campaign spending. Their research draws on surveys of candidates in Chicago-area cities of different sizes, and they differentiate between cities of fewer than 10,000 residents, 10–25,000, 25–50,000, 50–75,000, and more than 75,000. They show that it takes more money to win elections in larger cities, but with the exception of email (which is more commonly used in larger cities) tactics do not necessarily change. The major determinant of changes in campaign strategy is the city's median income. Counterintuitively, candidates spend less money in cities with higher median incomes than lower ones, and they are more likely to spend their money on email than on door-to-door contacts, flyers, mailings, or yard signs. Oliver and colleagues do not control for competitiveness or race.

Studies such as these reinforce a basic pattern of representational bias in local elections but show that the bias may be affected by features of the cities and the candidates – by the idiosyncrasies of particular elections, by whether the candidates raising the money are incumbents or nonincumbents, by city size, and by the city's racial composition. They suggest, furthermore, that what matters in local elections may be the ability of candidates to reach a threshold amount of funding. Beyond a certain point, additional fundraising may make little sense either because there are limited uses for the money or there is a very limited donor base. They suggest that urban campaign finance resembles the financing of other elections but that the smaller scale introduces some variations in how useful money is. All of these studies save for Oliver, Ha, and Callan's, however, are based on data from large cities, and their study solely considers cities smaller than those we consider here.

1.1.2 Campaign Contributions and Political Inequality

Second, there is an extensive literature on political participation at the urban level; such literature is often focused on voting although it at times includes other forms of engagement. The unit of analysis in this approach would be the individual donor, not the candidate. Much of this literature documents inequalities in voting patterns, the structuring of electoral conflict, and the representation of different groups in elected office. Kaufmann (2004, 41–44), for instance, notes that city politics tends to be structured by the city's demography, its economy, and the history of group control over the electoral process. Many cities have had longstanding political monopolies – decades or more of political control by a small group of individuals, often from the same ethnic background – and these monopolies have established patterns of "winners" and "losers" through the provision of benefits to particular groups (Trounstine, 2008). Because most city elections are nonpartisan, it is to the advantage of political leaders to structure politics around ethnic group identities – and, given the lack of partisan cues, voters very well might do so anyway.

Two features of urban elections tend to depress turnout: nonpartisan elections and off-cycle elections. Nonpartisan elections can deprive citizens of partisan cues, and they also remove traditional issues of partisan contestation from campaigns (Schaffner, Streb, and Wright 2001; Martin, Adams, and Lascher 2024). According to the National League of Cities, only seven of the nation's thirty largest cities hold partisan elections, and the majority of these seven cities are so overwhelmingly Democratic that there rarely is serious competition in the general election.[3] Hajnal (2009, 140), Anzia (2014), and Hartney and Hayes (2021) have all shown that holding municipal elections in odd-numbered years can depress turnout by thirty percent or more. As a consequence of these two features, turnout in municipal elections often is less than thirty percent of the electorate in major cities. Furthermore, Oliver, Ha, and Callan (2012) have shown similarly low voter turnout in smaller cities.

Those who have studied urban elections generally agree that low levels of voter turnout have led to a bias in representation against racial minorities and against the less wealthy and less educated. Hajnal (2009) notes that while most national studies of differential voter turnout in state and federal elections have discounted the idea that voter turnout is linked to policy outcomes, the disparity in turnout in urban elections is so great that that assumption must be rethought. Schaffner, Rhodes, and La Raja (2020, ch. 6) show substantial bias in policy outcomes against minorities and the less wealthy; they contend that the gap in preferences between whites and nonwhites is a far greater predictor of policy outcomes than are structural features such as nonpartisan or off-year elections. They show, furthermore, that whether a city uses at-large or district-based representation for its city council has a similarly small effect compared to the disparity in attitudes by race. This stands in contrast to the assumptions made by those who have argued for the abandonment of at-large representation (e.g., Behr 2004; Collingwood and Long 2021).

---

[3] See www.nlc.org/partisan-vs-nonpartisan-elections/.

Most of these studies focus on voting, and most of the data for these studies (except, again, for Oliver, Ha, and Callan's work) come from analyses of larger cities. All have clear implications for the study of campaign finance. Campaign contributions are a form of political participation. Given that a political contribution is more costly than a vote, contribution data should show greater biases toward the wealthy than do voting studies. The absence of partisan cues may have implications for campaign finance – while contributors may well be a sufficiently aware group of individuals that they know the partisan or ideological inclinations of candidates, incumbency, race, or ethnicity may play a role in encouraging contributions. And the nature of the electoral system may also have implications for who gives – district-based systems, for instance, may constrain the donor base more than at-large ones. And, following Schaffner et al. and Hajnal, greater disparities in political attitudes between whites and racial minorities may be related to contribution patterns.

1.1.3 Campaign Contributions, Political Parties, and Election Systems

Third and finally, the same variations in election laws and government structure that make it hard to consider large, cross-city datasets on campaign finance can be a virtue in that we can explore the effects of election procedures that exist at the urban level but not (yet) at other levels of government. These include innovations in campaign finance laws, proportional or ranked-choice election systems, and nonpartisan elections.

Older work on urban campaign finance often called attention the variations in election laws or campaign finance regulations. For instance, Fleischmann and Stein's (1998) study of St. Louis and Atlanta, two cities of similar size but with different types of governments (weak mayor, partisan elections and strong mayor, partisan elections respectively) is intended to measure the relationship between these two systems and the propensity for candidates to raise funds from outside the city or from particular types of business interests. Austin and Young (2006) analyze campaign spending and contribution sources in Toronto, which has strict contribution limits, and Calgary, which does not. Krebs (2004) provides a similar comparison of corporate and labor contributions in Los Angeles, a city with contribution limits, and Chicago, which does not have limits. Gierzynski (2007) compares spending levels and election results in Albuquerque, which has had a public financing component, to those of similar cities that do not have public financing. And Malbin and Parrot (2017) compare elections in New York, which has a public financing system, to Los Angeles, which does not.

Three cities in particular have drawn the attention of campaign finance scholars because of the implications of their campaign finance and election laws for national debates over reform. In 2020 Washington, DC adopted a public financing system that consisted of an initial block grant to qualifying candidates, followed by a match of $5 for every dollar contributed by small donors. Holman's (2021) analysis, comparing the 2020 election to prior Washington elections, showed that most candidates for city office abided by the terms of the program, that the program appears to have benefitted a diverse range of candidates and equalized spending in competitive races. The donor pool, furthermore, was less wealthy and more racially diverse than in prior years.

Seattle adopted a voucher program for city council elections in 2017. Seattle residents were given four $25 vouchers they could confer upon the candidate or candidates of their choice; those candidates could then redeem them for campaign expenses. Heerwig and McCabe (2019) and McCabe and Heerwig (2019) compared Seattle elections before and after the establishment of the voucher program and showed that while voucher use was more common among wealthier, better educated residents, the program did make the pool of contributors somewhat less unequal than was the pool of donors before the program. Yorgason (2024), however, demonstrates that those most mobilized under the voucher program belong to groups already overrepresented within the donor pool.

In 2009 New York adopted a system of public financing that featured a six-to-one match for candidates who agreed to a range of restrictions on fundraising and expenditures. Two major studies – one by Kraus (2011) and another by Malbin and colleagues (Malbin, Brusoe, and Glavin 2012; Malbin and Parrot 2017) have sought to compare New York elections before and after the implementation of the public financing system. While Kraus is skeptical that the system has changed election outcomes, Malbin and colleagues show a substantial increase in small donations in New York council elections. This is, they note, a consequence not only of donors feeling empowered by the six-to-one match but of candidates actively soliciting contributions from residents whom they might otherwise ignore. These studies limit consideration to a particular city or (in the case of the Malbin and Parrot 2017 piece) pair of cities in order to control for the city's culture and political history and to focus instead on the effects of the change in campaign finance law.

New York has also drawn attention because of the implementation of ranked choice voting (RCV) in the city's Democratic primary in 2021. RCV or variants of it were used in 22 American cities of varying sizes during the mid-twentieth century; research conducted on those cities' elections showed that RCV enhanced the representation of minority groups while at the same time leading to the election of councilors with stronger educational or professional backgrounds (Barber 1995, 2000). Contemporary research also shows, however, that local elites successfully organized to repeal such laws in most cities (Santucci 2022). There is no accessible campaign finance data from the time so one can only speculate about RCV's implications for the donor pool or for the funding of different types of candidates. Over the past decade, however, RCV has been adopted again in a range of cities, including Minneapolis, Oakland, San Francisco, Richmond (California), and Salt Lake City, as well as several smaller cities. Recent research has suggested that RCV might be able to reduce political polarization, improve the quality of campaigns, or enhance minority representation. All of these suggestions have implications for candidate fundraising and for donor contribution strategies, yet little research to date has focused on this relationship. The fact that New York, the largest city to use RCV so far, also had recently adopted new public funding laws makes it difficult to separate the effects of the two things in looking at its elections (Schmitt 2021).

The studies of Washington, Seattle, and New York show the potential for local reforms to influence debates at the national level, and they show the importance of developing a large body of information on the financing of urban elections. We can show, for instance, how elections in Seattle changed with the implementation of vouchers, but we cannot determine whether Seattle's idiosyncrasies as a city mean that such proposals would yield similar results in other places. We can compare New York and Los Angeles elections to understand how public financing influenced New York elections, but we cannot necessarily determine whether the size of these cities produced different results than what we would see in smaller places. Answering these questions can produce important information for those who would use these cities' models as building blocks for reform in other cities or at the state or federal level.

Finally, an old innovation in municipal elections – the absence of party labels, endorsements, or primaries – can also inform broader discussions. Nonpartisan municipal elections were, along with off-year elections, Progressive Era reforms aimed at insulating municipal politics from the influence of political parties (Abrams 1964). Some contemporary reform advocates have proposed nonpartisan primary or general elections at the state and federal levels as ways to decrease political polarizations. Yet students of political parties have noted that polarization still occurs in nonpartisan contexts and that parties tend to find ways to organize even in nonpartisan contexts (Masket and Shor 2015). Scholars of party networks often use patterns in campaign contributions, and the signaling effect of contributions from particular party leaders, elected officials, or interest groups, as a way to demonstrate the existence of "shadow parties" or factions. Such networks are perhaps more likely to exist at the local level than at the national level, as it is easier to signal one's position in a network in smaller, more tightly knit communities (Makse, Minkoff, and Sokhey 2019; Santucci 2022).

Collectively, these studies present a paradox – America's largest cities exhibit substantial inequalities in political engagement of all sorts, including campaign contributions. Yet cities also exhibit such a wide range of different election laws and campaign finance practices that they can provide important ideas for policy change. The bias in all of this research toward larger cities, however, means that we lack a full picture of how local campaign finance laws work. Addressing this gap has important implications not just for providing an accurate picture of American urban life, but for how we can think more generally about how to use campaign finance information to improve American politics.

2 Four Midsize Massachusetts Cities

Massachusetts cities are not, to be certain, representative of all midsize American cities; they have a different political culture and distinctive election laws that should be taken into consideration. Nonetheless, the cities we select as cases in Massachusetts share features with midsize cities across the nation, most especially, as we describe below, Worcester, Lowell, and Springfield.

Like many midsize cities in the Rust Belt and Midwest, Springfield, and Lowell were once manufacturing hubs that faced economic decline as industries moved away. In recent years, they have been working, like many others, to revitalize through investments in education, healthcare, and technology. Worcester (home to Clark University, Worcester Polytechnic Institute, and the University of Massachusetts Medical School), Springfield (Western New England University, Springfield College), and Lowell (University of Masschusetts - Lowell) all benefit from their higher education institutions, similar to how universities shape economies in other university-based towns. Cambridge, being adjacent to Boston, is something of an outlier in this group, but as the home of Harvard University and the Massachusetts Institute of Technology it is similar to upscale, highly educated cities with top universities in places such as Austin, Texas, Madison, Wisconsin, and Berkeley, California.

These Massachusetts cities have also seen growing immigrant and racially diverse populations. And while they are denser than midsize cities in the South, they are geographically similar to those in the Midwest and they face housing affordability challenges that align with national patterns in older industrial cities with economic struggles. While Massachusetts tends to be more Democratic, liberal, and wealthy than most states, these cities like many others face significant challenges with economic inequality, public school funding, and educational outcome disparities.

As in many midsize cities, Massachusetts municipal elections are non-partisan. They also feature a process that resembles party primaries and serves to winnow the number of candidates to two competitors for each position. In three of the four cities considered here (all but Cambridge), preliminary elections for council districts are held when there are more than two declared candidates. In the case of at-large elections, the field is winnowed in the preliminary election to twice the number of at-large council slots. Preliminary elections are thus not held in every cycle, but when they are they take place on the second Tuesday of September in odd-numbered years. The general election is held on the first Tuesday in November of each odd-numbered year. Cambridge stands out among these cities for its use of STV elections to choose the council.

One obvious reason we look at cities in Massachusetts is because the data exist thanks to a state law requiring standardized campaign finance reporting to be submitted to the state agency regulating money in politics. We are also residents of the state and know its cities especially well. We are all too aware of the analogy of "searching for keys under the lamppost" to criticize research that focuses only on areas where data is available, suggesting that this approach leads to biased conclusions. However, creating some empirical foundations where data are available is a solid first step to jumpstart additional research. Moreover, even if the data are limited to certain contexts, it can still reveal important patterns, trends, and potential causal mechanisms that may apply more broadly. Finally, we do not blindly generalize about our findings. We are careful to assess whether the mechanisms at work are likely to operate similarly in other contexts. And we acknowledge limitations of our analysis as we describe the results, even as we explain how the findings might extend beyond the immediate cases.

Table 1 compares the relevant characteristics of these cities, and it offers a summary of our expectations of how these characteristics might shape fundraising by candidates and contributions by individual donors, parties,

Table 1 City Characteristics and Expectations

	Cambridge	Lowell	Springfield	Worcester
Constant Attributes				
Size	118,403	115,554	155,929	206,518
Partisanship (Biden Vote 2020)	92.0	65.8	72.6	68.3
Variable Attributes				
Election Rules	All council members run at-large in STV election; mayor chosen by council	Mixture of at-large and district seats; mayor chosen by council	Mixture of at-large and district seats; mayor runs independently for four-year term	Mixture of at-large and district seats; mayor serves on council but elected by voters
Strong Mayor	No	No	Yes	No
Election Rule Changes	None	Switch from all at-large to mixture, with majority–minority districts, 2021	Switch from all at-large to mixture, with majority–minority districts, 2009	None
Racial Composition	66.0% white 16.7% Hispanic 10.7% Black	60.3% white 17.3% Hispanic 12.5% Asian	45.0% Hispanic 31.2% white 20.9% Black	51.8% white 23.4% Hispanic 11.9% Black

Median Family Income	$147,492	$89,761	$54,646	$71,265
Local Media	Boston Media	Newspaper, no TV	Newspaper and TV	Newspaper, no TV
Expectations				
Candidate Fundraising	High, consistently	Low except for 2021	Low except for 2021; variation in mayoral years	High, variable
Incumbency Advantage	Variable	High, except in 2021	High	High
Minority Candidates	Low	Low, except in 2021	High	Low
Outside spending	High	Low	Low	Moderate
Parties/Groups	Active	Less active	Less active	Active

Sources: U.S. Census data 2020; Presidential vote from Massachusetts Secretary of State.

and groups. These expectations shape the analysis that we will provide in the remainder of our analysis. A more detailed narrative summary of recent political events in these cities is available in Online Appendix A.

Even in this four-city comparison where many features are held relatively constant, there are simply too many factors in play to scale or prove that one factor causes a particular pattern of fundraising. Our research design does not permit strong causal inference. Nonetheless, we approach this analysis with several informed expectations rooted in the existing literature. First, while money may matter less in local elections than in national contests – due to lower media costs and limited voter engagement – we still expect it to play a meaningful role in shaping who runs and who wins, particularly in competitive or contested settings (Oliver et al. 2012; Anzia 2022). However, we anticipate that its impact is limited overall, given the low-information nature of many municipal elections and the limited salience they hold for most voters (Oliver et al. 2012; Schaffner et al. 2020). That said, we expect that nonincumbent fundraising will be positively associated with electoral performance, reflecting a well-established pattern from higher-level contests (e.g., Jacobson 1980; Canon 1993) and supported by recent findings in local elections (de Benedictis-Kessner 2018). Campaign funds likely signal viability to voters and enhance candidate visibility – both of which are crucial in low-salience settings.

We also expect that institutional variation will shape patterns of campaign finance. District-based elections may facilitate more targeted fundraising and potentially widen access to donors, while citywide or at-large systems may favor better-known or wealthier candidates who can mount broad campaigns (Trounstine and Valdini 2008; Trounstine 2018). In cities using ranked-choice or proportional systems, such as single transferable vote (STV) in Cambridge, we anticipate that campaign dynamics – including donor pools – will differ modestly, possibly attracting candidates with broader or more ideologically diverse support (Amy 2002; Donovan et al. 2016). Similarly, governance structures may matter: cities with strong mayor systems could concentrate political and fundraising power in the executive branch, while weak mayor or council-manager systems may disperse resources and elevate council contests (Svara 1990; Clarke 1998). We expect moderate differences here, but we are cautious in drawing hard conclusions. We are also able to explore the effects of changes in election systems because two of our four cities, Springfield (2009) and Lowell (2021), switched from at-large election systems to a hybrid systems to hybrid systems with majority minority districts.

Finally, and most importantly for our purposes, we approach our analysis with the expectation that local political context and structure shape the nature of political competition and campaign finance. Even in officially nonpartisan elections, we anticipate relatively stable factional patterns – particularly in cities with long-standing ideological or interest-based divides. When politics is organized more clearly around racial coalitions than around ideology, we expect different dynamics of donor mobilization, particularly with regard to who contributes and which issues dominate campaign narratives (Benjamin 2017; Trounstine 2018). Lastly, we anticipate that interest groups will play a meaningful but not overwhelming role in campaign finance, especially in low-turnout, low-visibility contexts where their resources can be deployed strategically (Anzia 2022; de Benedictis-Kessner and Gaudette, working paper). These expectations guide our inquiry into the patterns of money, organization, and power in midsize city politics.

3 The Candidates

We are able to compare candidates of different types in these four cities over time, in order to determine whether, for instance, incumbents outraise nonincumbents, white candidates outraise nonwhite candidates, or whether city size, wealth, or election system is related to particular types of fundraising practices.

Massachusetts has relatively strict campaign finance rules compared to other states, and the state's Office of Campaign and Political Finance (OCPF) makes data for state and some local elections easily available. Candidates running for city council seats in cities of more than 100,000 residents (for the duration of this study, Boston, Cambridge, Lowell, Springfield, and Worcester) are considered "depository" candidates.[4] All receipts must be deposited into a designated depository account, and all expenditures must be made from it, using a special check provided by the OCPF. Periodic reports are filed by the campaign with the bank, which forwards the information to the OCPF. Data on contributions are thus easily accessible and searchable for these cities.

Contributions to state and local candidates may not exceed $1,000 per year per individual (or in the case of joint checks $2,000 per couple). Contribution limits were doubled in 2015 from $500 to $1,000. When the

---

[4] Following the 2020 census, the threshold for depository candidates was lowered to 80,000; as a consequence, municipal candidates from eight other Massachusetts cities are now also required to file with the state.

candidate deposits a contribution, he or she also files the contributor's name and address with the OCPF. Contributions under $50 do not need to be itemized in this way and may be combined into a single deposit unless a contributor's aggregate, nonitemized contributions to a candidate or committee exceed the $50 threshold in a calendar year. Political action committees (PACs) are held to a $500 per year limit on contributions to a depository candidate or their committee but have no aggregate limit. Local party committees are limited to $1,000 per year in contributions per candidate while state party committees may contribute up to $3,000 per year. All contributions from business corporations are prohibited, although unincorporated businesses may be used to make contributions, provided they are attributable to an individual proprietor of that business and are applied to their individual contribution limit. Candidates may contribute unlimited funds and make unlimited loans to their campaigns.

Prior to 2011, district-level candidates were not required to file with the state, although some cities required candidates to file reports with the city, and the city made these reports available on its website. In contrast to the city-wide candidates, candidates who file with the city but not the state are not required to file their data electronically. While state-level filings can easily be sorted or converted into spreadsheet format, those who file with the city submit reports on paper, which are then scanned by the city and made available as .pdf files. While we have total fundraising amounts for these candidates, then, we were unable to analyze data on individual contributions. A change in Massachusetts law for the 2011 election, however, required district candidates to file with the state.

The data we use in this Element are thus drawn from OCPF contributor records for at-large municipal candidates from 2005 to 2021, and for district candidates from 2011 to 2021. We combine these data with election returns and candidate-level variables such as race, gender, or incumbency status. We also used markers provided by the OCPF to identify contributions from PACs, party committees, or candidate committees (other than the candidate receiving the funds). We hand coded some of these contributions as well to ensure accuracy, and we identified contributions or loans from the candidate receiving the funds. We also hand coded contributions from within the city where the election was taking place and outside, assuming that aggregated unitemized contributions and any other contributions without an address connected originated from within the city. Contributions were aggregated for each contributor/recipient pair (that is, if one donor gave three $50 contributions to the same candidate, we itemized this as one $150 contribution).[5] These data have enabled us to generate annual, city-specific tables that show relationships between fundraising and election results.[6]

Contribution summaries were checked against the candidates' post-election disclosure forms to ensure accuracy. We do not, however, consider candidate expenditures, which may be significantly higher or lower than the aggregated contribution totals, and we do not take into account candidates' carryover balances across elections, which may also be substantial at some times. Finally, while Massachusetts has since 2010 required the disclosure of independent expenditures to the OCPF, we do not include independent expenditure data in our analyses of candidate fundraising or donor characteristics, but we do summarize independent expenditures in our consideration of interest group activity (Section 6).

3.1 Sources of Candidate Funding, 2005–2021

Variations in the structure of city government make it difficult to present merged data on patterns over time. Hence, Table 2 shows average receipts for different types of candidates in each city over the full 2005–2021 time period, and Figures 1 through 4 show city-by-city trends over time for different types of contributions (note that the totals and averages are not inflation-adjusted). Figure 5 shows the relationship between receipts and votes for at-large incumbents and nonincumbents in the non-STV cities (that is, all but Cambridge). And Figure 6 shows the relationship between receipts and votes in district elections in Springfield and Worcester, the two cities with such elections for more than one election during this period. This table and these figures serve as the basis for our discussion below of each city; following these discussions we offer some broader conclusions.

First, let us briefly summarize the salient patterns in these figures. Table 2 shows that, as one might expect, incumbents raise substantially more than nonincumbents. Incumbent fundraising is much higher in Cambridge than in the other cities, and it is lowest in Lowell. Although averages can be skewed by individual candidates (as in Cambridge or Springfield) or

---

[5] Transcription errors, minor differences in form completion and other factors can make it difficult to correctly aggregate contributions from a single donor within and across campaigns. To improve our accuracy, we use a networks-based estimation of unique political donors that more robustly identifies individual and household donors by taking advantage of pre-cleaned name and address information simultaneously. For more information, see Rolfe et al. n.d.

[6] For a full summary of these annual reports, see https://wordpress.clarku.edu/rboatright/worcester-campaign-finance/worcester-campaign-finance-project/.

Table 2 Average Fundraising by Candidate Type and City, All Years Combined

City	Candidate Type	Mean Receipts	Standard Deviation	Minimum	Maximum	N
Cambridge	Incumbent	70,405	56,388	11,541	392,100	71
Cambridge	Nonincumbent	20,750	19,723	100	85,653	98
Cambridge	Incumbent Losers	88,101	89,562	—	—	8
Cambridge	Nonincumbent Winners	42,865	16,808	—	—	16
Lowell	Incumbent	14,181	8,008	1,300	38,990	69
Lowell	Nonincumbent	11,269	11,015	57	66,535	83
Lowell	Incumbent Losers	13,379	4,531	—	—	10
Lowell	Nonincumbent Winners	16,171	14,471	—	—	17
Springfield	Incumbent	23,469	36,375	1,135	185,012	96
Springfield	Nonincumbent	12,089	21,817	25	176,145	78
Springfield	Incumbent Losers	33,331	—	—	—	1
Springfield	Nonincumbent Winners	22,324	9,687	—	—	6
Worcester	Incumbent	30,933	41,980	600	354,221	77
Worcester	Nonincumbent	13,793	14,015	100	55,998	83
Worcester	Incumbent Losers	28,811	12,809	—	—	8
Worcester	Nonincumbent Winners	32,723	13,033	—	—	9

Money, Partisanship and Power in Local Politics 25

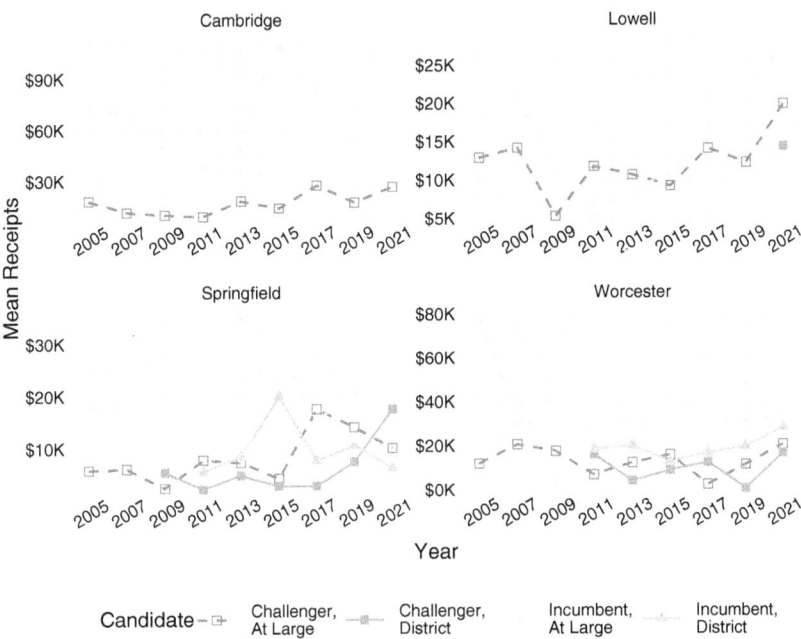

Figure 1 Receipts by Candidate Type, All Four Cities, 2005–2021

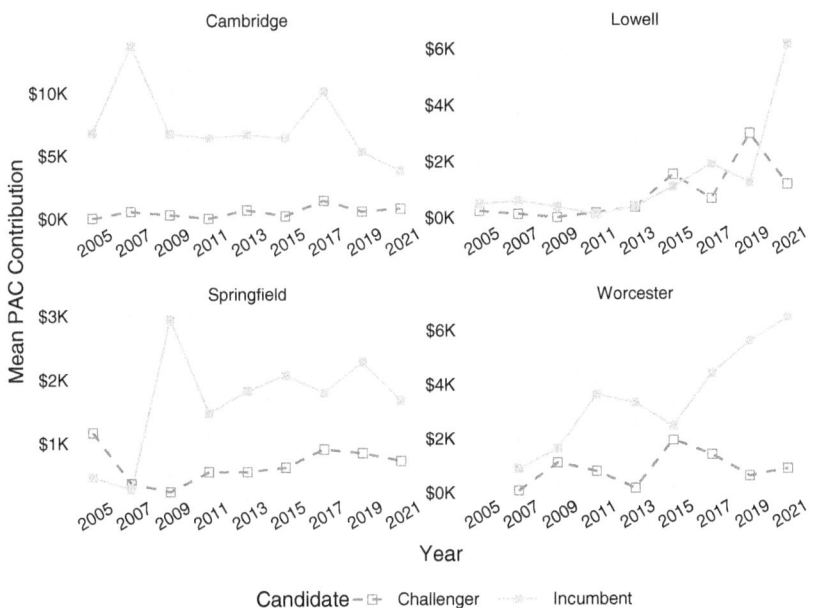

Figure 2 Mean PAC Receipts, All Four Cities, 2005–2021

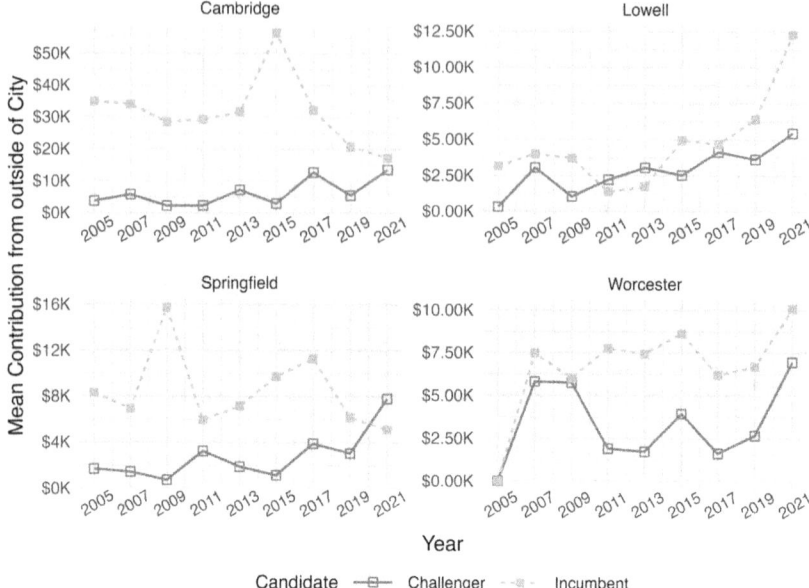

Figure 3 Mean Receipts from Outside of City, All Four Cities, 2005–2021

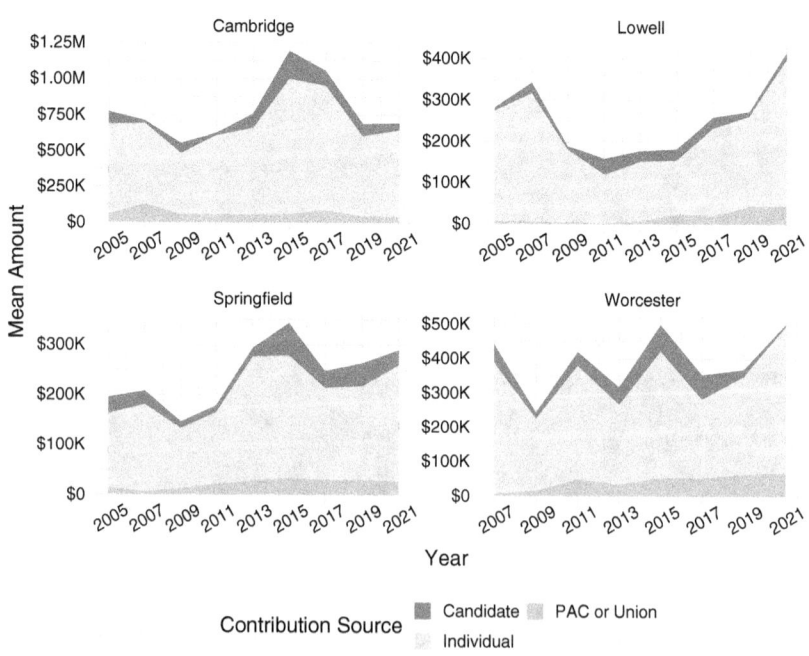

Figure 4 Cumulative Contributions by Donor Type, All Four Cities, 2005–2021

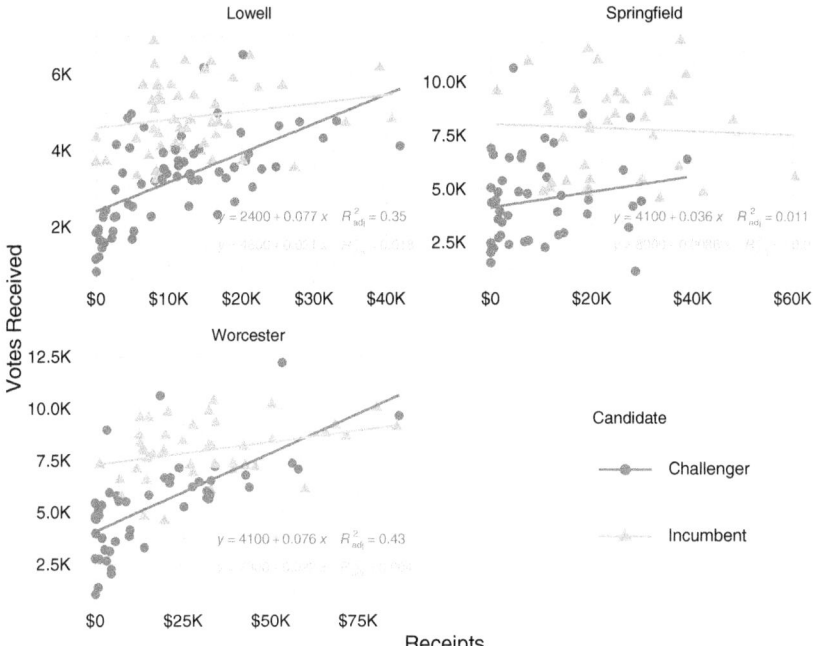

Figure 5 Receipts by Number of Votes, At-Large Candidates, Lowell, Springfield, and Worcester

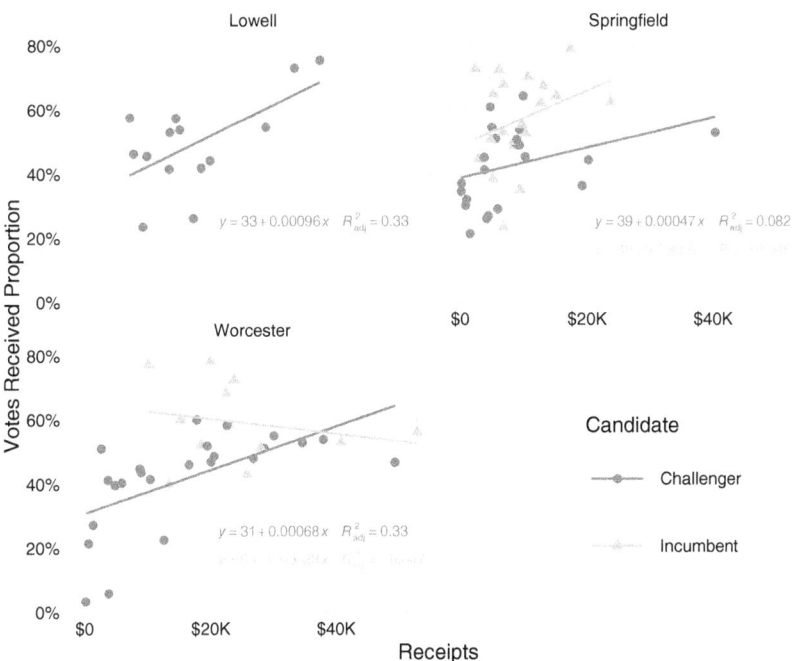

Figure 6 Receipts by Number of Votes, District Candidates

election system changes (Lowell), Figure 1 shows that there has been no obvious increase over time in candidate receipts. PAC receipts (Figure 2) have increased for incumbents in three of the four cities, although they still comprise a low percentage of total fundraising (Figure 4). Although nonincumbents raise less money from outside the city than incumbents (Figure 3), there has been an increase in the amount of money nonincumbents raise from outside the city in three of our four cases.[7] Figure 4 also shows that there has been an increase in the total amount of money raised from outside of the city. Figure 5 shows that fundraising is a much better predictor of nonincumbent fundraising than it is for incumbent fundraising; in each of these cities there are some at-large incumbents who win despite raising almost no money. When we exclude uncontested races, however, Figure 6 shows that fundraising is correlated with vote share – although there remain some incumbents who face no opponent and raise little or no money. We exclude Cambridge from these final two tables because its STV system makes analysis of vote share difficult.

3.1.1 Cambridge

Cambridge and Worcester are the only two cities considered here that have not changed their election system during the 2000s. All Cambridge elections for the 2005–2021 time period have been for at-large council seats, conducted using STV. Because Cambridge is also two to three times as wealthy as the other three cities under consideration, it is difficult to determine whether it is Cambridge's election system or its wealth that makes its election financing different. Yet Table 2 shows that Cambridge elections are substantially more expensive than the other cities. The average Cambridge incumbent during this time period raised $70,400, more than twice the average in any other city. While each city had one or two very high-spending outliers, it is also noteworthy that the minimum spent by a victorious Cambridge incumbent was $11,500. Each of the other three cities had several incumbents over this time period who spent negligible amounts of money – the minimum in each of those three was below $2,000. While one might attribute the high spending in Cambridge in part to the city's wealth, the absence of incumbents who can campaign based on name recognition alone seems likely to be a consequence of the city's ranked choice voting laws. No incumbent can expect to win merely by turning out

---

[7] We only consider individual contributions here, and we note that some of these cities have suburbs, so some out of city contributions may come from people who live adjacent to the city or have business interests there.

his or her reliable supporters, and the uncertainty about outcomes induced by the STV system may well push all candidates to campaign more aggressively than they would in a plurality system.

Cambridge also exhibits a much larger gap in average spending between incumbents and nonincumbents than do other cities. When one excludes candidates who raised no money, incumbents spend over three times as much money, on average, as nonincumbents. The gap is nowhere near as large in any of the other cities. This is in part a reflection of the absence of uncontested incumbents who raise little money, but it also suggests that despite the STV system, Cambridge elections are not necessarily any more financially competitive than those of the other three cities. As Figures 1 through 3 show, there is a wide gap between incumbents and nonincumbents in receipts, PAC contributions, and contributions from outside the city. There are some anomalous incumbents who raise large sums of money, but there are fewer anomalous nonincumbents than in the other cities.

With the exception of the spike in spending in 2015, driven by one candidate who raised slightly under $400,000, there is a greater level of stability in Cambridge than we see in the other three cities.[8] This is shown in Figure 4. Overall spending in Cambridge elections has not increased over the past two decades. Although there are some individual candidates with support from outside the city, there is no trend over time toward greater involvement in elections by individual donors from outside the city.

A final point of comparison between Cambridge and the other cities is a consideration of incumbent losers and nonincumbent winners. The point of this is to determine how easy it is for nonincumbents to win a seat on the council and whether vulnerable incumbents recognize themselves to be in danger and raise money to ward off opposition. Or to put matters in other words, in a plurality system that elects, for instance, the top six finishers, some incumbents may believe themselves to be safe and hence raise little money while others see themselves as likely to finish sixth or seventh and thus may raise substantial sums of money. Table 2 compares candidates who fall into these two categories within each city. In the three plurality systems (be they at-large or district-based), defeated incumbents raise as much as the average incumbent – in other words, incumbent losers do not necessarily raise extra money in order to protect themselves, but they also do not obviously lose because of poor fundraising. Nonincumbent

---

[8] This is Leland Cheung, a candidate who had run unsuccessfully for Lieutenant Governor in 2014. As is the case for some other outliers in our data, he may have been raising money for other campaigns during this time. Cheung had raised $67,000 and $77,000 in his two prior campaigns.

winners, however, are different in Cambridge than in other cities. In all three plurality cities, nonincumbent winners are arguably successful because of their fundraising – they raise as much or more than the average incumbent. In Cambridge, in contrast, nonincumbent winners raise less than sixty percent of what the average incumbent raises.

While we cannot conclude for certain that the high cost of elections in Cambridge is a consequence of the STV system – it may instead reflect the city's higher average wealth or proximity to the very expensive Boston media market – the different patterns in incumbent and nonincumbent fundraising seem more tied to the nature of the voting system. We might generalize this to say that there is less job security for incumbents in an STV system – all incumbents need to campaign, while in a plurality system some incumbents do not. And successful nonincumbents do not win because they are the obvious focal point for donors – money does not flow to one or two candidates who look strong enough to knock off incumbents. A moderately well-funded nonincumbent also has a better chance of victory in an STV system than in a plurality system, particularly if that candidate has a clear ideological, racial, or ethnic identity. Hence, while overall money appears to matter more in the STV context, it matters more for incumbents but less for some nonincumbents. As we will see in Section 5, some of this uncertainty can be mitigated through the development of slates.

3.1.2 Lowell

Lowell has had some contentious elections over the past twenty years, but these elections have not necessarily been symptomatic of enduring ideological or racial cleavages within the council or the electorate. Prior to the 2021 change to district-based council elections, however, there is little evidence that conflict has an influence on fundraising. As Figure 1 shows, the average incumbent raises only slightly over $10,000, and the average nonincumbent raises only slightly less. There is no correlation between incumbent expenditures and votes, although there is a positive and significant correlation for nonincumbents (see Figure 5). Some long-tenured incumbents have gone for years without raising more than $6,000 or so, although there is only one incumbent over this time period who did not report raising at least $3,000. The spike for nonincumbent spending in 2007 was driven by one candidate who raised $66,000 in his successful campaign for office.[9] The spike in average candidate receipts

---

[9] As an incumbent, that candidate raised only $15,000 in the subsequent election, and lost.

in 2021 – the first election with the new combination of at-large and district seats – suggests that the exclusively at-large composition of the council, perhaps coupled with the absence of a mayoral election, may have diminished the importance of money and created more stability in fundraising over time. The sums of money spent are not necessarily anomalous; Lowell is approximately half the size of Worcester and its at-large incumbents raise approximately half as much.

Similarly, receipts by donor category are relatively consistent across election cycles, as Figure 4 shows; with the exception again of the anomalous candidate in 2007, contributions from the candidates, from political committees, and from city residents are relatively consistent over time until 2021, although there is a slight secular increase in out-of-city contributions.

The 2021 election is significant for understanding campaign contributions, then, because of its forced reallocation of council seats. Figure 4 shows that the change to a hybrid system did not change the sources of contributions, and voting statistics show that voter turnout also did not increase significantly in 2021. The election did significantly change the average amount of money raised. This could be a consequence of establishing competitive district races. However, this could also be a one-time occurrence. Five of the nine at-large incumbents ran in three different districts, driving up the cost of those races, and the remaining five districts had competitive races between nonincumbent candidates. There were preliminary elections in four of the city's eight districts in 2021, and three of these four did not have a preliminary candidate who received a majority of the vote. This circumstance is unlikely to be repeated in subsequent elections. For instance, there were no preliminary elections in Lowell in 2023, and the evidence from Worcester's district elections and Springfield's ward elections suggest that most district incumbents face little opposition.

Some news articles from the time of the election, however, identified enduring cleavages within the districts, among ethnic groups or on socioeconomic lines, so competition may persist in some parts of the city but not others. There is little evidence of partisan cleavages in Lowell – no news coverage of the city races suggests there are candidates who draw on a network of Republican donors as was the case in Worcester. But the votes for Cambodian candidates who ran for at-large seats prior to 2021 suggests that these candidates had much more concentrated support than white candidates (*Lowell Sun 2013*). The competition among Cambodian candidates in 2021, furthermore, was often quite bitter, suggesting that there are distinct network of voters and donors within the Cambodian community (Ebbert 2022). As we shall see in subsequent sections, however, the establishment of majority minority districts can actually broaden candidates' fundraising bases – if it was clear that a Cambodian candidate was going to win the election in particular district, then donors who may otherwise not have contributed may decide to give those candidates a second look.

3.1.3 Springfield

Springfield changed from an at-large system to a hybrid system in 2009. Because Massachusetts did not require ward-level candidates to file reports with the state until 2011, this highly competitive election year is not fully captured in our data. The candidate averages for Springfield show, however, that with the exception of the particularly uncompetitive 2021 election, at-large councilors raise roughly twice as much as ward incumbents (Figure 1). As is the case in Lowell, there is no relationship between votes and receipts for at-large incumbents (Figure 5) although there is a positive relationship for nonincumbents. In ward races, there is no relationship between receipts and votes for either incumbents or nonincumbents (Figure 6). The scatterplots in Figure 6 remove two outlier candidates; the time series in Figure 1 does not, so the influence of these candidates can be seen in the 2017 averages.[10]

Returning to the earlier four city comparison figures, Figure 4 shows few signs of changes in contribution sources over the past decade. As in the prior tables, 2017 is unusual because of the funds raised by one candidate. Although the 2009 data are not reliable in this figure – they include only the at-large candidates and the small number of ward candidates who voluntarily filed with the state – comparing the 2005 and 2007 data to the data from 2011 onward shows that if there was a change in contribution sources in 2009, it was not sustained after that election, and that Springfield's hybrid system elections did not draw more contributions than they had before 2009.

Springfield is the least wealthy city among those considered here, and much of the news coverage of its elections notes concerns over very low turnout, particularly in the city's poorest neighborhoods. Although the shift to ward elections in 2009 led to substantial turnover and to gains in minority representation over the subsequent three election cycles, campaign spending has been particularly low among the council candidates and is unrelated to the election outcome. Mayoral candidates in Springfield

---

[10] This candidate was Thomas Ashe, who also ran for Hamden County Sheriff during his election cycle.

(not included in our data because the mayor is not a councilor) traditionally raise well over $100,000 and attract substantial amounts of money from outside of the city. The Springfield mayor has greater power than the mayors of the other cities discussed here, both formally and informally. Yet the separation of the mayor from the council may serve to diminish the role money plays in council races.

3.1.4 Worcester

Worcester elections are perhaps the most stable of the four cities considered here; the city did not change the structure of its council or its election format during the time period covered here. As a consequence, it is easier in Worcester than in other cities to understand changes over time with reference to individual candidates or to the politics of individual elections. Data on elections to the six at-large council seats (including the mayorship) are available for the full 2005–2021 period, while data on district elections are available from 2011 to 2021.

Figure 1 shows average receipts for incumbent and nonincumbent at-large candidates. With the exception of the 2005 election, in which the city's mayor (who is also a councilor and is therefore included in our data) raised money that could subsequently be used for a statewide run, the pattern in fundraising is relatively consistent. The average incumbent raises between $20,000 and $30,000 per election cycle; roughly two-thirds of this money is raised within the city. Political committees overwhelmingly favor incumbents. There is a relatively weak correlation between fundraising and electoral success for incumbents; once a candidate has raised a threshold amount of money, there is little evidence that subsequent fundraising increases vote totals. In 2019, for instance, one successful candidate raised only $1,200 while there were two unsuccessful candidates who raised over $30,000. Mayoral races have, however, been contentious at times, and the highest-spending incumbents tend to be mayoral candidates. This is not surprising, given that this is a citywide election that attracts the most attention from voters. Mayoral candidates also tend to raise substantially more money from outside of the city and from PACs than do other council members. The successful mayoral candidate has raised over $50,000 in each of mayoral election since 2013; in 2007 an unsuccessful mayoral candidate raised over $80,000.

On average, nonincumbent at-large candidates lag far behind incumbents, although there is substantial variation among nonincumbents. Nonincumbent winners, as we will discuss more in detail later, tend to outraise incumbents. Figure 5 shows the relationship between receipts and vote share for incumbent and nonincumbent candidates; as the scatterplot here shows, the correlation between receipts and vote share is not particularly high within either group, but the slope for nonincumbents is steeper than it is for incumbents, indicating that nonincumbents benefit more from strong fundraising than do incumbents. The same is true for contributions from outside of the city (not shown). Jacobson (1978) has demonstrated this same dynamic in federal elections, suggesting that the marginal dollar spent by challengers provides voters with more information, including elevating name recognition relative to the well-known incumbent.

Apart from mayoral races, these elections are marked by a substantial degree of stability over time. Given the small number of candidates in each of these cycles, variations are often caused by individual candidates. For instance, in 2015 one candidate (who ran successfully for council but unsuccessfully for mayor) invested $45,000 of his own money in the race; in 2021, one successful nonincumbent candidate for city council used ActBlue and invested heavily in social media advertising to raise over $55,000 overall and $22,000 in contributions from outside of the city.

We only have data for district races from 2011 to 2021. There is much greater variation across districts and over time in these races. As Figure 1 shows, incumbent district councilors tend to raise less than incumbent at-large candidates. This is not a function of lower prestige or smaller district size; rather, it is a consequence of a lack of competition. District councilors running unopposed (forty percent of those included) rarely raise above $15,000, and in some instances unopposed district councilors raise less than $5,000. There is no "warchest" effect as there is for higher-level legislative office. When there are credible opponents, however, district council races can feature multiple candidates who raise $20,000 or more, and who raise extensive funds from PACs or from out-of-city contributors. And when there are open seats or competitive challenges to district incumbents in the city's wealthier neighborhoods, spending by incumbents and challengers alike exceeds average spending in at-large races. Figure 6 also shows a scatterplot of incumbent and nonincumbent district candidates; it shows that there is no correlation at all between receipts and vote percentage in these elections.

Returning to the figures comparing all four cities, let us now consider the total amounts raised by election cycle as opposed to the average candidate receipts we considered earlier. We use the period from 2011 to the present to ensure that contributions to at-large and district candidates are included. Figure 2 shows that contributions from political organizations – which mostly consists of labor unions and the campaign committees of state legislators – have provided a consistent but small percentage of contributions over the past several elections. Candidate contributions or loans are sporadic, but Figure 4 shows that there is no clear trend toward larger or smaller expenditures by the candidates themselves. With the exception of a sharp drop in 2017, however, it does seem evident that contributions from individual donors (see Figure 3) within and outside of the city have been increasing since 2013. One might attribute this to particular candidates or particular district elections. However, there are also noteworthy shifts among individual donors.

To summarize, Worcester differs from the other cities considered here in that it has a relatively conventional electoral system that has been unchanged for the 2005–2021 time period. Over this time, campaign finance has been relatively consistent. Although some incumbents win elections despite raising little money, most incumbents raise a threshold amount of money each cycle. Fundraising is weakly tied to electoral success, but it is more important for nonincumbents. In district races, incumbents tend to raise money if they are threatened but otherwise do not raise very much money. Most spending is driven by competition in the city's mayoral race or in instances where district seats are open or district incumbents appear to be vulnerable. There appears to be a slow trend toward greater spending overall in city races, a trend reinforced by more fundraising outside of the city. These patterns mirror dynamics at the federal and state levels: nonincumbents depend more on money for success, competition spurs fundraising, and increasingly donations come from outside the jurisdiction. The latter may be facilitated by greater use of fundraising platforms like ActBlue, which lowers the transaction costs of reaching wider audiences.

3.2 Race, Gender, and Fundraising

Many studies of campaign finance at the state and federal levels have addressed the question of whether women and racial minorities are at a disadvantage in raising money (Kitchens and Swers 2016; Thomsen and Swers 2017; Grumbach and Sahn 2020). We have no particular expectations about whether the characteristics of these four cities might lead to differences in the ability of female candidates to raise funds. However, we anticipate that the racial composition of the cities might pose challenges for minority candidates in fundraising. To the extent that some contributors might prefer to donate money to people of the same race, cities with larger minority populations and with majority minority districts might produce some minority candidates who are able to draw on a donor base of the same race.

There are two challenges in making these comparisons, however. First, we have no reliable measure of candidate quality for municipal candidates, so a consideration of nonincumbent candidates may well pull in a range of different candidate types. When, for instance, there is a very small number of nonincumbent racial minorities running, we cannot reliably determine whether the candidate's race or ethnicity was the cause of a strong or weak fundraising performance. Second, the effects of race may be different depending on the racial composition of the city. It is difficult to guess whether, for instance, Vietnamese candidates in Worcester should be at a disadvantage compared to Hispanic candidates, whether African American candidates might have different fundraising prospects compared to candidates who come from an African immigrant community, and so on. We lose a lot of rich information when we make binary distinctions between white and nonwhite candidates. And, third, as noted earlier, many incumbents are secure enough that they do not have to raise or spend very much money at all, so if we observe, say, a Black incumbent who raises little money, we cannot determine whether that is a consequence of difficulties raising money or of a lack of effort to raise money.

Nonetheless, we can observe some patterns across the four cities. In regards to gender, women are more likely to win in all cities except Springfield, although the difference is only significant in Cambridge (2005 to 2011) and in Worcester from 2013 to 2021. Women in two of these cities (Worcester and Cambridge) substantially outraise male nonincumbents, while the reverse is true on Lowell and Springfield. However, in each of the four cities, male incumbents raise more than female incumbents by between 50 and 100 percent. Figure 7 shows differences by gender in each city. There is also significant variation for men, many of whom are people who self-funded their campaigns or raised money in the expectation of pursuing higher office. A 2024 study by WGBH noted that 35.6 percent of city council members in Massachusetts are women – a six-percent increase since 2019 – and that the percentage of female mayors had nearly doubled from twenty-one to forty percent (Cohan 2024). Despite this statewide increase in representation, we found no increase over time in receipts for female candidates.

Nonwhite candidates are less likely to win than white candidates in all cities except Cambridge, with a significant difference of thirty (Springfield) to forty (Lowell and Worcester) percentage points in success rates prior to 2013. In more recent elections, the advantage is no longer significant in any of the three cities, and the differences in success rate have virtually

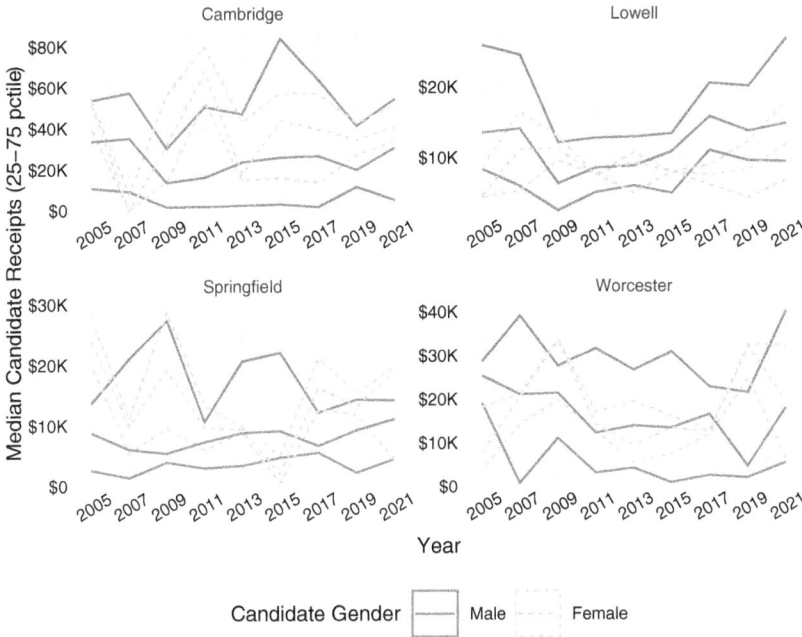

Figure 7 Average Receipts for Male and Female Incumbents Council Members, by City

disappeared in Springfield and are cut in half (to twenty percentage points) in the other two cities.

We initially created a four-category measure of race, in order to look at fundraising for Asian, Black, Hispanic, and white candidates, and we further distinguished between incumbents and nonincumbents. This distinction was somewhat useful in gaining impressionistic evidence about different cities – it helped us to note, for instance, that candidates of Asian descent actually outraised most other candidates in two cities (Cambridge and Worcester) but that these successes were largely a function of one or two very strong candidates. In the city with the largest Asian American population (Lowell), candidates of Asian descent, all of whom were Cambodian, ran well behind white candidates before the establishment of the two majority minority districts. The varying racial makeup of these cities also left us with very small numbers of cases; for instance, Lowell had no Black incumbents and only two Black candidates at all, while Springfield had no Asian candidates.

We therefore focus here only on incumbents, and we collapsed our race measure into two categories, for white and nonwhite incumbents. Our results are shown in Figure 8. This figure shows that there are no systematic differences in campaign fundraising by candidate race in Cambridge.

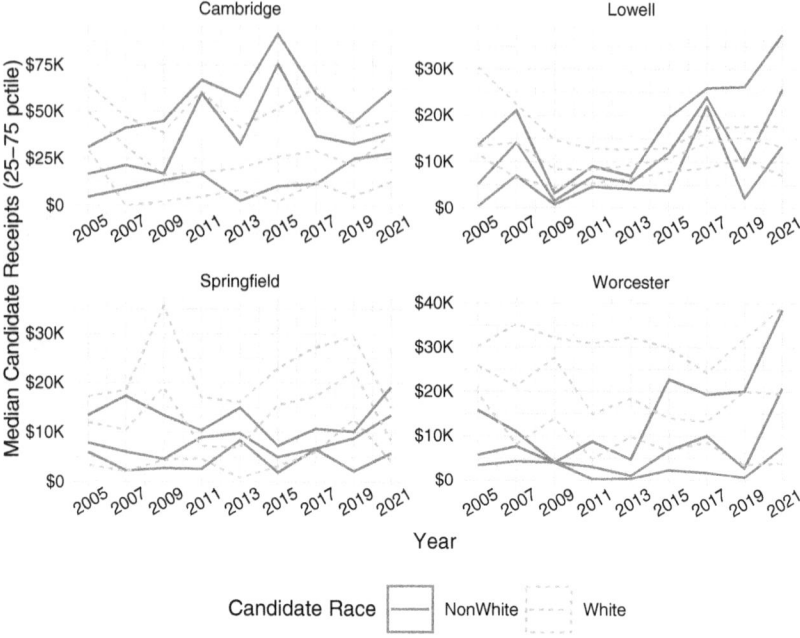

Figure 8 Average Receipts for White and Nonwhite Incumbent Council Members, by City

Lowell had a significant difference by race prior to 2013, with nonwhite candidates raising about half as much money as white candidates but this is not observable in later elections. In Springfield, nonwhite candidate fundraising barely shifts over the near two decades of elections, while white candidate fundraising doubles – resulting in a significant difference in more recent elections that does not translate into lesser success rates for the nonwhite candidates. In Worcester, racially linked candidate fundraising patterns are pronounced over the time period, although the fundraising deficit for nonwhite candidates decreases from almost $20,000 to $8,200. This disparity may be the result of majority minority districts, however – both Springfield and Worcester contain at least one incumbent who represented a minority district and raised close to no money after his or her initial victory.

3.3 Broader Lessons

Most research on campaign finance in the United States has considered federal and state elections. The cost of campaigns for these offices has increased dramatically over the past four decades, as a consequence of an increased reliance on advertising, increased partisan conflict, and changes in campaign finance law. In municipal elections, in contrast, the smaller scale makes these findings less relevant. Few municipal candidates advertise on television, and many municipal candidates are sufficiently well known that they do not need to campaign at all, or if they do, they do not need to spend money to campaign. In addition, municipal elections are often nonpartisan, which means that the stakes of these elections are lower and voter turnout is often lower as well.

The comparison here illustrates these patterns. Fundraising across all of these cities is remarkably stable over time. Where there are variations they are generally a consequence of clarifying elections at the mayoral level, which drive turnout precisely because they change the issues. The sources of funds are also very stable over time. The lack of a strong correlation between incumbent fundraising and vote share means that it is particularly difficult for nonincumbents to win elections. The few nonincumbents who are successful are generally far more dependent on money – particularly from donors outside the city and the traditional fundraising base for incumbents – than is typical for other candidates. In short, the absence of a relationship between money and votes makes for less competitive elections and ensures that a base of consistent donors is all that is needed for incumbents to stay in office.

The findings here corroborate many findings in studies of larger cities – incumbents tend to need a threshold amount of money to be competitive, and the donor base is skewed toward a small number of wealthy donors and toward particular types of interests. Other features of midsize cities seem noticeably different, however. The councils of these cities are smaller than those of big cities – the largest city council among these four cities has eleven members, much fewer than the city councils of Chicago (50) or New York (51). The small council size may mean that elections can be shaped far more by idiosyncratic candidates. The role of race is different as well – while race has traditionally played a dominant role in many big cities' elections, it is arguably less of a determinant of outcomes or a source of divisions within the councils of these four cities. Where it does matter, it matters in unusual ways given the particular characteristics of these cities' racial composition.

This comparison also provides suggestive evidence about difference in election systems and election systems change. Two cities considered here changed their election systems during the time considered here while a third uses STV, an election system that has attracted substantial interest from reform advocates nationally. The similar size of these four cities makes it possible to think about how variations in election rules work while controlling for other factors. The differences are instructive – in two cities, a change from at-large elections to district elections was accompanied by a substantial one-time change in candidate fundraising and expenditures. This change introduced uncertainty and made incumbents more vulnerable in the short term. However, that shift was not accompanied in either city with a change in voter turnout or an enduring change in campaign finance. Whatever merits the change to district-based elections had in these cities, there is little evidence from our data so far that it had a measurable long-term effect on where money comes from, on the incumbency advantage, or on the nature of campaigns. While there is much more work that would need to be done to further substantiate this claim, it does fit with what is known about election changes elsewhere at the state and federal levels. As we shall see in Section 4, however, the change may have increased the propensity of nonwhite citizens to donate to candidates, and it may have changed the fundraising strategies of nonwhite candidates.

The ranked choice comparison is also intriguing but requires much more evidence. We know from prior work that candidates are expected to think about campaigning differently in an STV system than they do in a plurality system (see, e.g., Amy 2002). Most of the claims made in this regard have to do with campaign rhetoric or how candidates target voters. It stands to reason that candidates would think about fundraising differently, as well. The comparisons here suggest that they do; however, we would need to explore who contributes, not just how much money is contributed, before pursuing this claim any further.

4 Donors

It is well known that campaign contributors in federal races are not particularly representative of the general public. We know that voters in local elections tend also to be unrepresentative of the general public – to be wealthier, older, and less racially diverse – so there is reason to believe that the biases in who gives in local elections are more dramatic than biases in federal elections. Apart from some contributor surveys, however, there is little evidence to support this claim. In this section we document these disparities; we show that there are biases but we also show that the donor base varies significantly across elections and it is driven in part by who runs in local elections.

We address both of these issues by matching campaign contribution records for Cambridge, Lowell, Springfield, and Worcester against descriptive data on individuals taken from the Catalist database. In this section we describe what we know about local campaign contributors and their partisan or ideological behavior.

4.1 Campaign Contributors in Municipal Elections

It is well established that campaign contributors at all levels are unrepresentative of the general population. From this point, however, there are many comparisons one could make. First, one could compare all contributors to the general public, or compare contributors in local elections to contributors to other campaigns. Hajnal (2009), Hajnal, Kogan, and Markarian (2022), and others have shown that voters in local elections tend to be wealthier, older, and less racially diverse than those cities' full electorates or than voters in state and federal elections. Schaffner, Rhodes, and La Raja (2020) have shown that local elected officials differ from their constituencies in these same ways. Given that local elections tend to have lower voter turnout than federal elections, one might ask whether donors in these elections are even less representative of the public than voters or federal campaign contributors.

Second, one paradigm in the study of federal campaign donors is the distinction between "pushed" and "pulled" money (Malbin 2003). Some donors give habitually because they want to shape policy, while others are drawn into the system by candidate solicitations. Francia et al. (2003) draw on survey data to show that contributors to congressional campaigns tend to give habitually and to operate within social networks that remain somewhat consistent across elections. Such donors push money into the system. Magleby, Goodliffe, and Olson (2018), however, draw on Cooperative Election Studies survey data for the 2008 and 2012 elections to show that there is in fact substantial variability in the presidential donor pool across elections. Their study indicates that there is more "pulled" money, particularly from small donors, than previously assumed. This study may indicate that candidate characteristics matter in shaping the donor pool, but it may also show that the widespread adoption of internet giving since 2002 made it easier for new donors to appear. We can study this in considering local elections by exploring the change in descriptive characteristics of donors across elections.

Third, another contention in the literature on urban voting and campaign finance is that nonpartisan elections limit citizen engagement. Hajnal (2009) contends that the loss of partisan cues means that citizens with low levels of information are less likely to be involved; people who have lived in the same part of the city for longer will be more likely to vote and to be contacted by candidates. Adams (2010) shows that most municipal elections are characterized by a consistent pattern of out-of-city contributions – approximately one-third of total candidate fundraising – from individuals or organizations with financial interests in these cities. Adams' work considers variation in contributions across zip codes. Use of Catalist data can provide more detail on voter characteristics of relevance here such as occupation, income, or length of residence.

And fourth, the Francia and Magleby studies both contend that people who contribute different amounts of money to candidates have different motivations. Other contributor studies, such as La Raja and Schaffner (2015), have argued that small donors tend to be as ideologically extreme as large donors. At the federal level, many small donors seek out candidates with distinctive ideological or descriptive traits even if these donors do not reside in the same state or district as the candidate. Despite this, many advocates of greater campaign finance regulation celebrate small donors as being more representative of the general public, and they may well be in ways other than ideology. Literature on small and large donors has tended to focus on candidates – on who excels at raising money in different amounts – but we are also able to explore the donors themselves, by comparing characteristics of small and large donors and in-city and out-of-city donors.

In sum, existing literature has compared urban voters to their cities' full electorates and citizenry; it has compared federal campaign contributors to the full electorate; it has considered variations in motivations for small and large donors; it has considered the effect of partisan labels on elections; and it has explored changes in the donor pool across time. Comparing the demographic traits of municipal campaign contributors can help us understand whether there is bias in the pool of local donors. Comparing changes in the composition of the donor pool over time can show us whether donors push their money into the system or are drawn in by candidates. And comparisons of large and small donors can help us to understand whether donors are drawn into the pool for different reasons. Prior survey-based research has tended either to focus on federal elections or on particular large cities; here, our Catalist method enables us to compare cities and to gather more accurate information about donors than other studies of municipal elections have done.

4.2 Gathering Data on Campaign Contributors

To conduct this study, we matched Catalist data on race, ethnicity, age, length of residence, income, and ideology (as defined by Catalist's ideology model) to each donor in these four cities. We were able to successfully match over 85 percent of the name–address pairs in the contributor dataset, yielding a total of approximately 44,000 observations for the four cities. It is important to note that the error rate in matching donors into the Catalist database increases the further back one goes in time. We are confident that comparisons of donor attributes within each recent election cycle are accurate, and we are confident that measures of short-term variation between recent years (for instance, between 2019 and 2021) are accurate, but we have less confidence in time trend comparisons going back more than a decade.

The Catalist ideology model is constructed using more than 1.6 million survey responses to a battery of over 200 questions that were collected in the period between 2016 and 2020. Through a series of linear regressions using variables from the Catalist database, the model estimates the propensity of any given voter to hold progressive or conservative views, on a scale from 0–100 where 0 represent the strongest propensity of holding conservative views (and to identify as conservative), and 100 represents the strongest propensity of the individual to hold progressive views (and to identify as progressive). In this model, middle scorers are more likely to identify as moderate, but they may also express inconsistent policy views that render them unable to be ranked as having a consistent propensity toward one side of the ideological spectrum. Individuals may also rank in the middle due to a lack of relevant data.

4.3 Who Gives in Massachusetts Municipal Elections

As a first step in our analysis, we consider the characteristics of donors in these cities, whether the donor population is different from the broader voter population and the city population, and whether we can observe patterns among donors – patterns that reveal commonalities between small (or large) donors, or patterns that reveal relationships between donors that belie an informal "party" network.

We offer four sets of tables: summary statistics on changes over time in the composition of the donor pool within each city; yearly snapshots of variation by race and gender among different types of donors (breaking the donor pool into small, medium, and large donors, and into in-city versus out-of-city donors); estimates of the average age of different types of donors by year; and estimate of the average ideology of donors by year.

The first set of figures, Figures 9 through 12, show that in many ways the donor pool in each of these cities is relatively static. The proportion of large, medium, and small donations does not change dramatically across elections, nor do the basic characteristics of small and large donors

(Figure 11). Some cities exhibit a small increase in very small (under $25) donations over time, though we should treat this finding with some caution because online contributions became more common over the course of this time period and small online contributions are more likely to be reported as distinct contributions than are cash or check contributions to candidates (which may be reported as part of aggregated unitemized donations). In most of these cities, the proportion of women contributing to candidates increased slowly but steadily during this period Figure 10). This trend reflects a pattern in federal and state elections as well, as women increase their status and wealth in U.S. society. The four cities vary in the proportion of donors who reside within the city; it is common in Cambridge and Springfield for more than half of the donors to reside outside the city, while in Worcester and Lowell approximately one-third of the donors live outside the city (Figure 12).

The most noteworthy descriptive change in the donor pool in these cities is the increasing number of contributions by racial minorities (Figure 9). Some previous studies (e.g., Cho 2001, 2002; Adams and Ren 2006) have used surnames to proxy for ethnicity; this can perhaps work for some groups but not all. Catalist provides probability estimates of race which have been shown to be highly reliable (Fraga 2018, 222–226). We are able

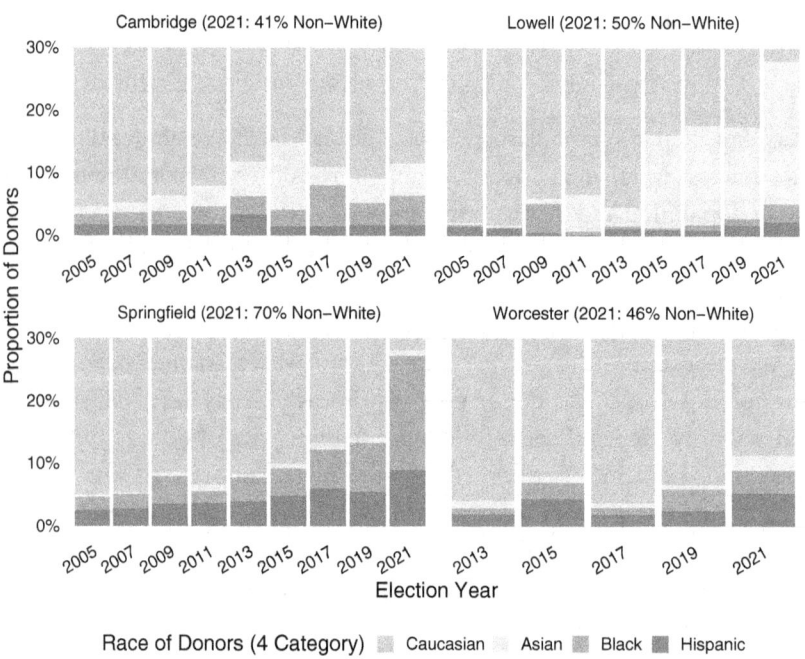

Figure 9 Donor Race by Year, All Four Cities

Money, Partisanship and Power in Local Politics   45

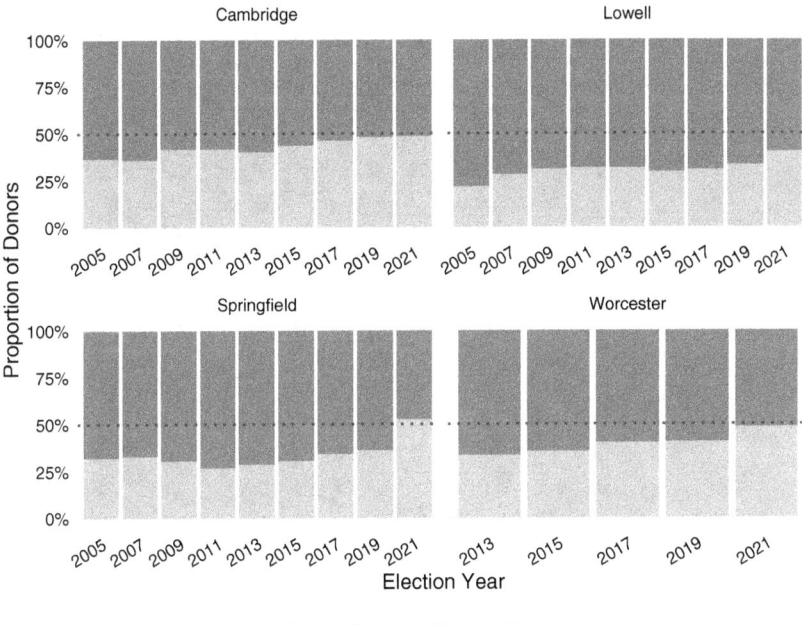

Figure 10 Donor Gender by Year, All Four Cities

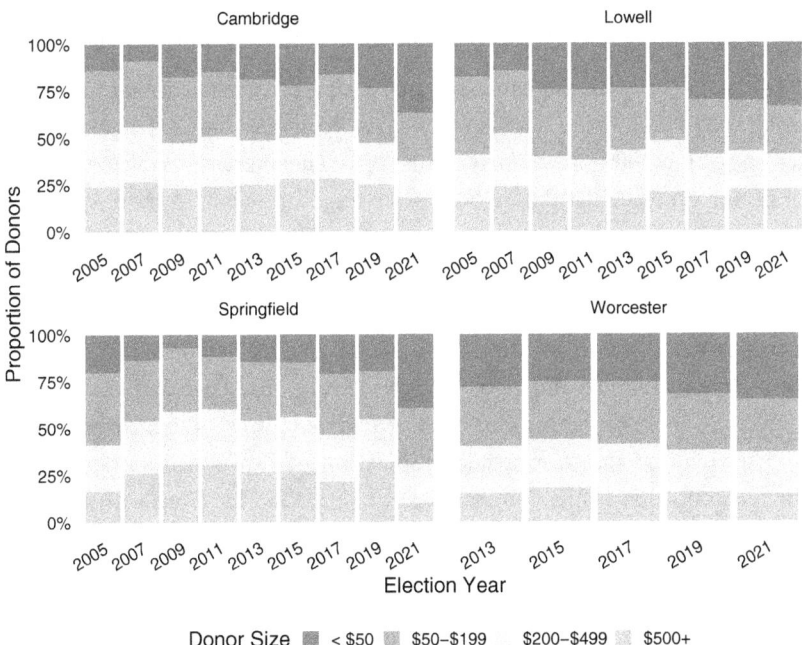

Figure 11 Proportion of Small and Large Contributions by Year, All Four Cities

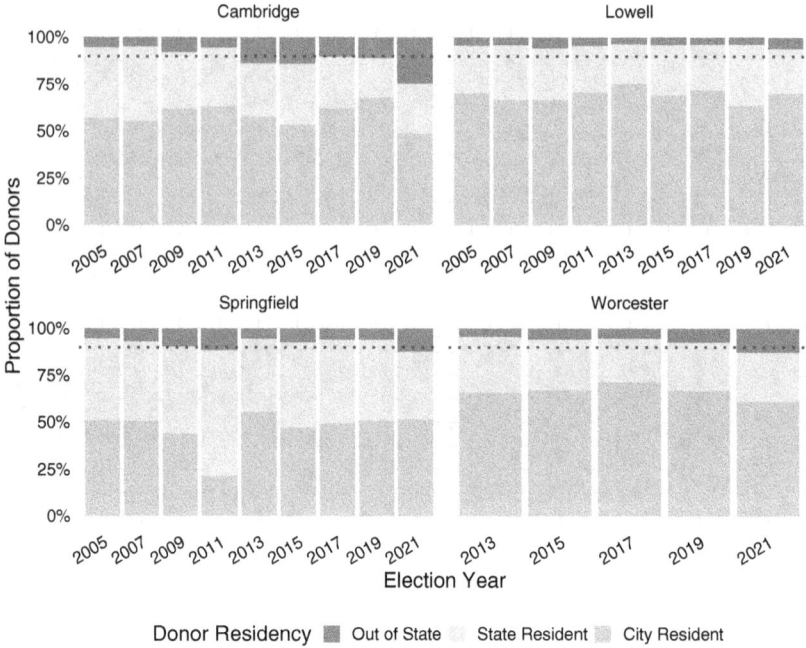

Figure 12 Donor Residency by Year, All Four Cities

to use these to estimate the probability that an individual donor is African America, Latino, Asian, or white.

Our data show that in Lowell, a city with a growing Cambodian population, people of Asian ancestry increased from less than 1 percent of the donor pool in 2009 to 27.4 percent in 2021. This increase occurred among all donor types; while the highest percentage of Asian American donors was within the medium donor category, the largest percent increase between 2019 and 2021 occurred among very large donors. There was also an increase in 2021 in the representation of Asian Americans among out-of-city donors, suggesting that these donors feel solidarity with Asian American candidates and give through identity-based networks.

Even given potential problems in Catalist matching for these early years, it seems evident that the racial composition of Lowell's donor pool has changed and that it has not necessarily changed in lockstep with changes in the racial or ethnic characteristics of residents themselves – there has been minimal change in the representation of other ethnic groups, and while today the percentage of Asian donors roughly matches the percentage of Asian residents, the Asian population has not increased at the same rate as the donor pool and was underrepresented as recently as 2013. Lowell had only two successful Asian American candidates before

2015 and did not have more than two Asian American candidates in any election year prior to this; since 2015, the city has averaged four Asian American candidates per year. In 2021, following the city's establishment of district-based elections, five Cambodian candidates ran; one won an at-large seat and the four others ran against each other in the two majority Asian districts. Increases in the representation of Asian donors precede the establishment of district seats (2021) as well as the increase in Asian candidates. As we will discuss in Section 5, the change from an at-large system to a hybrid system allows for more nonwhite donors to enter the core donor base, indicating that the candidates to whom nonwhite donors give are also supported by white donors, likely outside of the district.

Springfield, the city with the largest Black population of these four, has experienced an increase in the percentage of African American donors over the last two election cycles, to the point that the proportion of Black donors in 2021 almost matched the proportion of African Americans in the city population. However, unlike the case of Asian donors in Lowell, the increase in African American donations does not occur until well after the change to a hybrid system. Hispanic residents are dramatically underrepresented in all four cities. For instance, while over forty percent of Springfield is Hispanic, Hispanic donors never represent more than eight percent of the donor pool. Worcester and Cambridge, the two cities with the largest proportion of white residents, have an overwhelmingly white donor base, even though both cities have had several successful nonwhite candidates in recent years. This suggests that there may be a threshold percentage of residents of any particular minority or racial ethnic group that is necessary before the proportion of donors of that group begins to increase.

Table 3 breaks down the donorate for Lowell, the city with the most substantial change in the composition of its donors. This table shows whether change in the donor base happens consistently across all levels of donations or according to the residence of the donors. Comparing the 2019 and 2021 donors shows that the increase in Asian donors in Lowell was most evident among small donors (those who gave between $25 and $199). Very large donors remained disproportionately white, and although there was a change in the racial composition of out-of-city donors, overall, donors who do not reside in Lowell were more likely to be white and male. The same general imbalance was evident in the other three cities (data not shown).

We used Catalist data to measure the racial composition of the contributors to each candidate. We can do this by comparing the proportion of contributions by white donors to white and nonwhite candidates, as

Table 3 Lowell Contributors by Donation Size, Race, and Gender, 2015–2021

Year	Demographic	All Donors	Donor > $500	Donor $200–$500	Donor $25–$200	Donor < $25	Out of City	In City
2021	Asian	27.4	14.3	11.7	34.6	9.9	15.2	34.0
2021	Black	3.4	4.8	2.0	3.4	4.6	5.6	2.2
2021	White	66.8	78.2	83.4	59.8	82.8	77.0	61.3
2021	Hispanic	2.4	2.7	2.8	2.2	2.6	2.1	2.5
2021	Female	44.6	29.8	37.0	47.0	52.7	42.3	45.8
2021	Male	55.4	70.3	63.0	53.0	47.3	57.7	54.2
2019	Asian	18.1	6.5	6.2	25.7	9.0	10.0	23.8
2019	Black	1.5	0.0	1.5	1.3	3.0	1.5	1.4
2019	White	78.2	93.5	91.2	71.0	81.7	86.4	72.2
2019	Hispanic	2.3	0.0	1.1	2.0	6.3	2.0	2.6
2019	Female	36.8	29.0	27.9	39.1	41.8	35.0	38.1
2019	Male	63.2	71.0	72.1	60.9	58.2	65.0	61.9
2017	Asian	19.46	9.0	7.8	23.13	22.9	9.59	23.2
2017	Black	0.96	0.0	1.1	1.01	1.2	0.58	1.1
2017	White	78.53	91.0	89.5	75.0	74.1	88.95	74.5
2017	Hispanic	1.05	0.0	1.6	0.86	1.8	0.87	1.1
2017	Female	35.54	16.0	26.0	37.55	48.3	27.67	39.0
2017	Male	64.46	84.0	74.0	62.45	51.7	72.33	61.0
2015	Asian	18.29	10.0	11.0	21.46	21.0	15.0	18.07
2015	Black	0.49	0.0	0.0	0.42	2.0	0.4	0.55
2015	White	80.0	90.0	87.9	76.88	75.0	84.2	79.74
2015	Hispanic	1.22	0.0	1.2	1.25	2.0	0.4	1.64
2015	Female	35.36	22.0	33.1	35.55	47.0	32.0	36.55
2015	Male	64.64	78.0	66.9	64.45	53.0	68.0	63.45

we do in Figure 13, or we can take a more fine-grain approach, looking at individual candidates. White candidates in Lowell, more so than in other cities, rely heavily on white donors, and while the number of nonwhite candidates is small in all years except 2021, these candidates rely on a large nonwhite donor base. With a single cycle under the new electoral system, it is hard to say whether such dramatic racial differences will remain. Springfield may offer some answers, as the city had a similar change in election rules in 2009; however, do recall that the proportion of white donors remains very high in Springfield. There is a clear decrease in

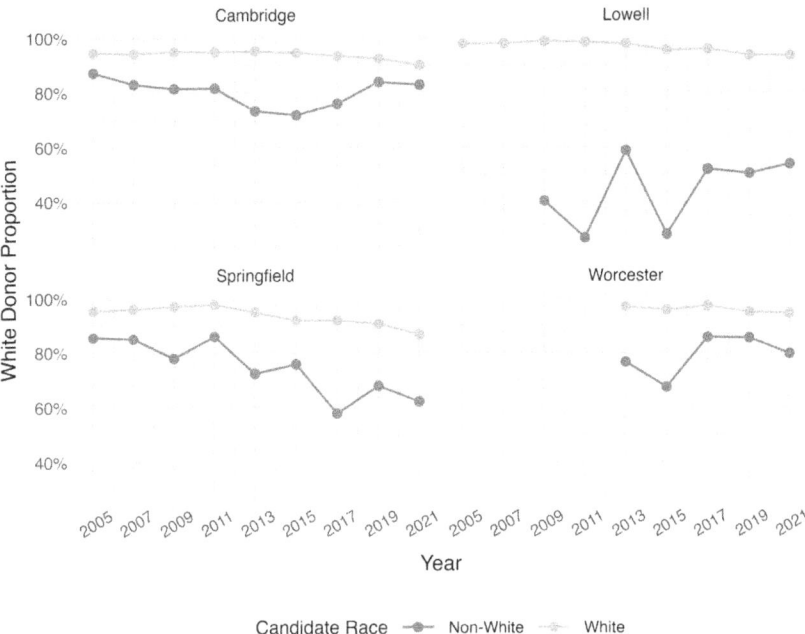

Figure 13 Proportion of White and Nonwhite Donors by Candidate Race and City

white donors giving to nonwhite candidates, and a much smaller decrease in white donors giving to white candidates. Worcester and Cambridge, the two cities with the highest proportion of white residents, tend to have quite white donor bases. In both cases, there is a slight decrease in white donors giving to white candidates, but the changes are minimal. In Worcester, there is a larger gap in white donors to white and nonwhite candidates, but there are no clear trends year over year. In Cambridge, while there were several years with lower-than-average donations from white donors to nonwhite candidates, the overall gap in white donors among white and nonwhite candidates is small in most years. Here again, the results of the Lowell redistricting make the city's contributor base stand out. The competitive Asian candidates in the city each raised a majority of their funds from Asian donors through the 2015 to 2021 time period, but the proportion of Asian donors to each candidate increased to over sixty percent of the total contributors to the three strongest Asian candidates in 2021. The proportion of white donors is very small – in some cases as low as twenty percent – in the predominantly Cambodian districts, which suggests that the city's largest donors were not trying to influence election outcomes outside of their home districts. However, the average nonwhite candidate did not become more reliant on nonwhite donors after the switch to district-based elections.

The racial composition of donors in Springfield is quite different. Successful Black candidates in Springfield tend to have a contributor base that is between twenty and thirty percent Black; for most of these incumbents, the percentage of Black donors declined once they had reached office. The increase in Black and Hispanic donors in 2021 (to a combined twenty-six percent of all donors) meant that two incumbent council members had a donor base that was more than fifty percent minority; interestingly, these two candidates were not newly elected but their donor base had become less white. Although Worcester and Cambridge had multiple successful minority candidates during these years, in each case these candidates' donors were more than sixty-five percent white. Nonwhite candidates were somewhat more reliant on white donors in these cities than in Lowell or Springfield but they still did have a more diverse donor base, on average, than white candidates.

Figure 14 shows changes in the average age of donors over time. Here again we see very slight changes in the donor pool over time. In all four cities, the average age of small donors declines slightly over this time period, while the average age of larger donors remains constant.

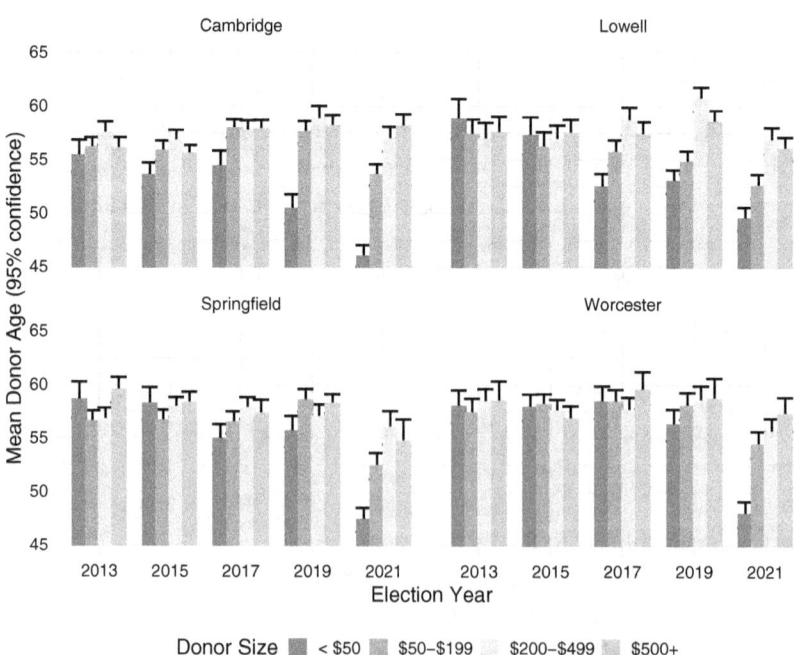

Figure 14 Mean Donor Age by Donation Size and Year, 2013–2021

Figure 15 shows the average ideology of donors over the past four election cycles, measured on a 0–100 scale where 100 is the most liberal. The averages by year change little, although the small changes we do see indicate movement to the left. In Cambridge, Springfield, and Worcester, the average ideology score for donors of all different contribution sizes increases modestly, while it remained constant in Lowell. Of particular interest, however, are the comparisons across donation size categories. There are no instances where the average donor in any category is to the right of center (that is, has a score lower than 50), but in almost every year and every city (except for Lowell), the average large donor is more conservative than the average small donor. This will be relevant in Section 5, where we consider the relationship between political ideology and donor networks.

It may strike the reader as unsurprising that the donors in these four cities tend to be quite liberal – after all, these cities are themselves quite liberal, as shown in Table 1, and although these elections are nonpartisan, most candidates espoused liberal themes and many have ties with the state or national Democratic Party. It is important to note, however, that there are many conservative residents in these cities. For Figure 16 we extracted Catalist data on the ideology of all city residents, and we compare the ideological distribution of donors – broken out by size of donation – to the overall population.

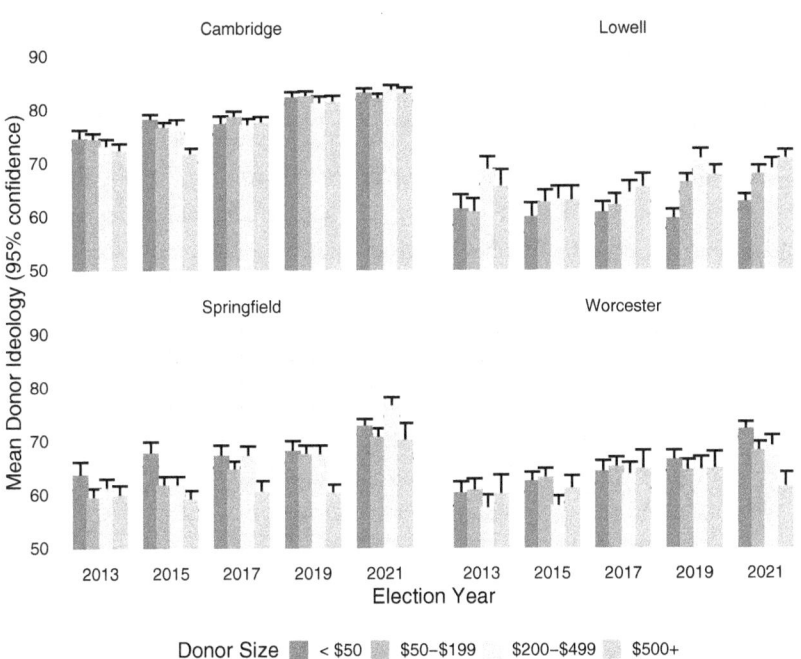

Figure 15 Mean Donor Ideology by Donation Size and Year, 2013–2021

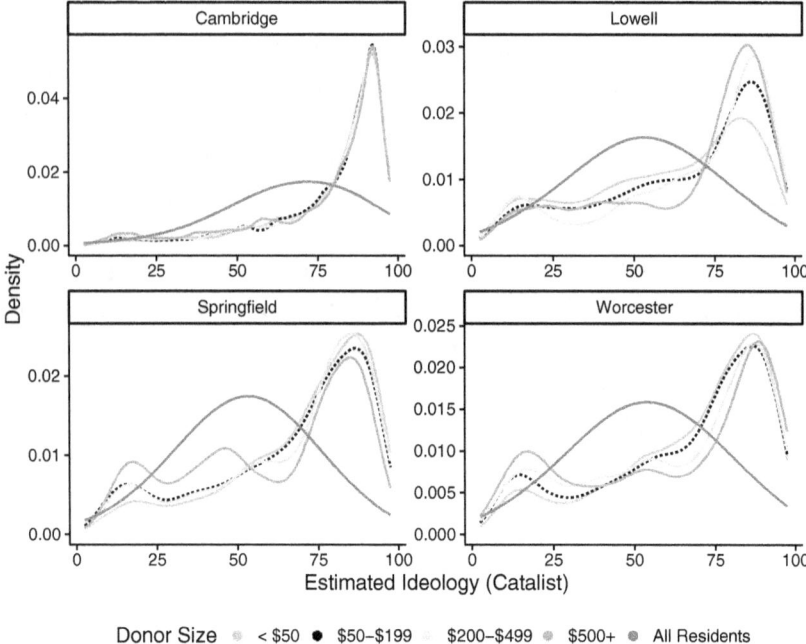

Figure 16 Donors and Residents Compared, 2015–2021

In all four cities, donors are substantially more liberal than most city residents. In three of the four cities, very liberal and very conservative citizens are somewhat overrepresented in the donor pool, while moderates are underrepresented. This is the pattern in contributions in federal races as well; there simply are not a large number of very conservative residents in these cities. So, even though conservatives are overrepresented among donors, they are not able to influence elections very much. Either the candidates they support tend to lose, or they give money to candidates who are much more liberal than they are. There are also a disproportionate number of conservative large donors, as compared to conservatives in the smaller donor categories. The lone city here without noticeable overrepresentation among very conservative voters is Cambridge, where the number of conservatives is vanishingly small. Even here, however, the proportion of conservative very large donors exceeds the proportion of conservative residents.

We conducted a separate analysis (not shown) of contributions by zip code. Adams (2010, 119) analyzes the geography of contributions in ten large cities, concluding that in most of these cities more than thirty percent of contributions come from the wealthiest ten percent of zip codes. In the smaller cities we consider, we do observe that three of the four have one or two dominant zip codes, that these zip codes are generally the wealthiest, best educated, and most white of the city zip codes, and that the zip codes with the highest percent of contributions also have the highest voter turnout. The lone exception is Springfield, which has much more variation in the origin of contributions. However, using zip codes is not particularly helpful in cities of this size. Although these cities have similar population sizes, the number of zip codes ranges between four and thirteen. This makes zip codes a much less useful proxy for income than is the case in larger cities – and, of course, we have individual-level measures of income to work with. We acknowledge that there may be contagion effects within neighborhoods – that geography may matter independently of income. This is difficult to measure, however, since individual candidates will have geographic bases, and in the cities with districts, the district lines will not necessarily correspond with zip codes.

4.4 Conclusions

In this section we have shown the possibilities that Catalist data provide for a detailed analysis of campaign contributors. We have highlighted differences between cities that seem to correspond to their racial and ethnic makeups and the nature of their electoral systems. These tables and figures show that there is substantial variation across these four cities – some show remarkable change across the time series, while others show great stability. They also show, however, that donors are not representative of their cities in terms of race, age, or ideology. The salient differences among these cities are that Lowell has an increasing Asian population and a new, as of 2021, election system; Springfield has a larger African American population and a larger number of African American candidates than the other cities; and Worcester and Cambridge have smaller minority populations and a much smaller proportion of nonwhite donors. As we shall see in the next section, however, this ideological consistency masks partisan conflict and polarization among donors.

5 Parties

Is competition in municipal elections structured by political parties? At first glance, the answer seems to be no. According to the National League of Cities, twenty-two of the nation's thirty largest cities hold nonpartisan elections for mayor and city council.[11] The remaining cities that do

---

[11] This is taken from a 2003 study (the most recent we could find) by the National League of Cities (MacManus and Bullock 2003). The fact that elections are formally nonpartisan does not mean, of course, that elected officials do not make their partisanship known. A tally by Ballotpedia identified 25 of these mayors as Democrats, three

hold partisan elections tend to be so Democratic that all of the meaningful competition takes place in the Democratic primary. Many urban elections are also held in odd-numbered years, in an effort to insulate them from partisan conflict at the national level.[12]

Works by Anzia (2022) and Oliver, Ha, and Callen (2012) have, however, drawn our attention to other ways that political parties and party-like coalitions might structure urban elections. Following Bawn et al. (2012), Anzia argues that formal political parties may not always play a strong role in local elections but that coalitions form among interest groups seeking to structure coalitions over time. Specifically, Bawn et al. (2012, p. 571) identify parties as "coalitions of interest groups and activists seeking to capture and use government for their particular goals." Under this definition of parties, candidates who are integrated into these broad networks stand a better chance at winning. Indeed, in U.S. Congressional elections, membership in a broad network of PAC donors significantly increases the electoral success of challengers (Desmarais et al. 2015). Further, delegates for national parties are highly polarized in their interest group memberships, which demonstrates that the most active members of parties rarely cross paths in nonparty activities (Heaney et al. 2012). These coalitional structures are like informal parties in that they subsume issue-related interest groups and other factions, drawing them into a long coalition that persists from election to election.

Using campaign finance data and a survey of municipal-elected officials, Anzia (2022) argues that formal political party organizations may exist alongside factional or issue-specific groups. Both formal and informal parties have reasons to support particular candidates, either because of the issue preferences of party members or out of concern for developing candidates for higher office in the future. Local formal parties, however, do not necessarily organize the activities of other local groups. Nor do they appear to structure conflict consistently in municipal elections and municipal policymaking the way they do at higher levels of government. Much of this organizing is left to allied interest groups, which form a separate party-like coalition.

Similarly, party-structured voting in the electorate is present but not pervasive (Hajnal 2009; Oliver, Ha, and Callen 2012). One important function of political parties is to shape voter turnout, sometimes restricting

---

as Republicans, and only two as independents or nonpartisans (see ballotpedia.org/List_of_current_mayors_of_the_top_100_cities_in_the_United_States).

[12] According to the Ballotpedia listing, sixteen of the thirty largest cities hold elections in odd-numbered years.

the voter pool to help favored candidates (Anzia 2014) or enlarging it (Oliver et al. 2012). Oliver and colleagues also find that the partisanship and ideology of elected officials in larger cities reflects the partisanship and ideology of their cities – that is, Democratic places tend to elect local officials with views consistent with those of national- and state-level Democrats, and the same goes for Republicans. Even in nonpartisan city councils in major cities like San Diego, elite party membership explains legislative coalitions (Burnett 2018). While there is little evidence of retrospective voting in local elections, Oliver et al.'s (2012) findings suggest that voters can make judgments about candidates' partisan inclination even without the cue of a party label. These voter decisions based on party preferences translate into policy preferences aligned with their own sentiments (Einstein and Kogan 2016; Benjamin and Miller 2019).

Much recent work shares a similar conception of parties as put forth by Bawn et al. (2012). They contend that (a) political parties are constructed by elites in order to organize legislative decision-making; (b) party coalitions are stable across elections; and (c) parties have programmatic goals – primarily shaped by groups in the coalition representing different subsets of voters.

Our contention is that we can identify informal local political parties – conceived of here as loosely organized factions that meet these three criteria – through network analysis of contributions. While in previous sections we identified types of donors in terms of demographic makeup, ideology, and so on, we can also think of networks of donors who interact directly, through mutual friends, shared email lists or social media groups, or through attendance at shared events. We use network analysis to identify the relationship of candidates to one another via mutual donor pools. Building on the constructed candidate networks, we further assess how candidate membership in emergent factions changes over time, how the factional donor bases differ, and whether faction members vary in terms of election outcomes or voting records.

Because local donors – particularly donors who give money to multiple candidates – can be construed as a political elite within these cities, our use of candidate networks meets the first criterion of a party (criterion a). We evaluate how stable candidate clusters are across elections (criterion b). We then match campaign contribution data onto data on donor ideology and race to determine whether the parties are differentiated (and stably differentiated), as further evidence to meet criterion (b) along the lines of criterion (c). Across all four cities, we find evidence that donor networks operate as informal parties. Winning candidates are drawn primarily from fairly stable factions, and these factions are often ideologically and racially distinct. The shape of partisan competition varies across the four cities: there is a unified single-party core in Springfield, stable two-party contestation in Cambridge, and a mix of a moderate single-party core and an emergent progressive party in Worcester and Lowell.

These clusters are not formal political parties, registered with a party name, although some are linked to formal party organization and prominent party-elected officials in the state. Loosely organized social clusters can provide cues to other elites, but only better organized formal associations (including those examined in the next section) are set up to provide cues to rank and file voters. However, loose-knit social clusters can and do provide stability over time, that is, long coalitions (Aldrich 1995), and can serve as the basis for understanding factions within city councils themselves.

We are also interested in the relationship between factional clusters and election systems. While all four cities we consider here are nonpartisan, their election systems vary in two ways. First, Lowell (pre-2021) and Cambridge hold only at-large elections, while Lowell (beginning in 2021), Springfield, and Worcester use a hybrid system. At-large elections are the most likely to encourage faction formation, due to the absence of one-to-one candidate competition and the greater uncertainty about election outcomes. On the other hand, just as at the national level, district-based systems may advantage geographically concentrated minorities. If the change to a hybrid system in Lowell is successful, we expect to see minority candidates entering a cluster of candidates that share a donor base. Springfield and Worcester also use hybrid systems, but their rules remain consistent over this time period.

Second, STV elections are considered by proponents to be a way to encourage compromise among legislators and to reduce polarization. If STV elections are doing this, we would expect less distinct party clusters in Cambridge than in other cities as candidates reach out beyond their core base and donors hedge their bets. Given the assumed uncertainty of electoral outcomes in STV systems, we would also expect to see less stability in emergent factions across elections (Santucci 2022). On the other hand, STV systems might incentivize political elites to organize the electorate and donors through clear signals as a way of increasing the odds of their favored candidates winning. We find evidence of the latter, which supports findings by Santucci (2022) about the uniqueness of Cambridge, which he attributes to the capacity of elites and voters to coordinate effectively. Cambridge has clearly defined political factions that are fairly stable across time and tightly linked to candidate endorsements made by rival community associations. We speculate that this is related to the high socioeconomic status of Cambridge voters who pay attention to cues generated by public slates.

5.1 Identifying Parties Using Campaign Contributions

To identify emergent local factions, we start by creating networks of candidates linked by shared donors for each election in all four cities. In other words, we reshaped contribution data into a network with individual candidates as vertices and donors as edges. In order for two candidates to have a tie, we required that they share at least ten donors in common. Setting the threshold too low, say at one donor in common, would allow a single donor to who donated to many candidates to single-handedly create network structure. The ten-person threshold does not allow one or a few highly active donors to artificially increase connections but is not too high to make it overly difficult for candidates to be connected in elections where the average winning candidate was supported by between sixty and two hundred donors. The overall structure of the resulting networks – density and transitivity of ties, plus proportion of isolates – confirms that the chosen threshold creates reasonable looking networks. We then classify candidates into potential factions supported by a shared loose-knit donor base using fast-greedy community detection to identify dense subgraphs (communities) within each network.

Table 4 shows network density, the proportion of isolates, and global and average local transitivity within each city by year. Density values describe the proportion of actual ties out of all possible ties, and generally range between twenty-five and fifty-five percent for traditional social networks (Rolfe 2014). The observed candidate networks in Table 4 follow a similar pattern, ranging from twenty-four to fifty-five percent of possible ties present when isolates are not included. The proportion of isolates is fairly high, with between fifteen and fifty-nine percent of candidates not having at least ten donors in common with another candidate, but this is to be expected as the data set includes nonviable or unrealistic candidates who received only a few donations, candidates who ran only in the preliminary election and raised less money, and incumbent candidates, particularly those running in district systems without opposition.

Transitivity is concerned with the structure of triadic relationships, which is critical to understanding loosely knit political factions. In an emergent faction, if candidate A has a tie with candidate B and candidate C, we would

Table 4 Network Descriptives, All Four Cities, 2015–2021

City	Year	Number of Candidates	Number of Communities	Proportion of Isolates	Global Transitivity	Average Transitivity	Density
Cambridge	2015	19	2	0.37	0.69	0.77	0.20
Cambridge	2017	24	2	0.46	0.57	0.70	0.12
Cambridge	2019	20	3	0.15	0.60	0.77	0.25
Cambridge	2021	18	2	0.28	0.55	0.64	0.21
Lowell	2015	18	3	0.28	0.75	0.81	0.28
Lowell	2017	23	3	0.22	0.68	0.77	0.23
Lowell	2019	22	2	0.23	0.72	0.85	0.32
Lowell	2021	24	2	0.12	0.70	0.75	0.31
Springfield	2015	27	3	0.59	0.71	0.83	0.08
Springfield	2017	24	3	0.54	0.56	0.71	0.07
Springfield	2019	26	3	0.42	0.46	0.68	0.08
Springfield	2021	22	3	0.55	0.73	0.72	0.06
Worcester	2015	23	3	0.48	0.35	0.62	0.08
Worcester	2017	21	2	0.57	0.61	0.82	0.08
Worcester	2019	19	2	0.47	0.61	0.71	0.12
Worcester	2021	18	3	0.17	0.57	0.75	0.23

generally expect there to also be a tie between candidates B and C. In Table 4, we can see that average local transitivity (or the density of each candidate's personal network, not including isolated candidates) ranges from sixty-two to eighty-one percent of connections between candidates B and C. Local transitivity weights individuals with smaller networks more heavily than global transitivity, which is simply the ratio of complete triads. Average local transitivity is systematically higher than global transitivity, ranging between thirty-five and seventy-five percent, which is consistent with the emergence of organized political factions where candidates are embedded in communities. Similarly, the identification of two to three candidate clusters in all elections across the four cities is consistent with the emergence of local factions.

In terms of overall structure, the biggest difference we observe across cities is the greater proportion of isolates in the hybrid council systems in Springfield and Worcester. As we discuss later, incumbent district representatives often do not face serious electoral threats and thus may raise fewer funds from a centrally connected political elite. The 2021 election system in Lowell does not include district incumbents, and thus it is unsurprising that viable candidates remain well connected to the core political elite.

Figure 17 shows examples of network structure in each of the four cities; networks diagrams for all cycles in all four cities are shown in Online Appendix D. Looking more closely at city-specific network structure, Cambridge shows clear evidence of two well-defined factions across all four elections, with an example from 2021 appearing in Figure 17. Drawing on local news coverage and community organization endorsements, we can describe these as a cluster likely to be endorsed by Cambridge Residents Alliance (prior to 2019) or Cambridge Citizens Coalition (from 2019), and a second cluster likely to be endorsed by A Better Cambridge. All incumbent candidates belong to one of these two factions, even in 2019 when a third faction briefly emerges. Of the fifteen candidates who run in multiple years and are assigned to a faction, only two switch between well-organized factions while two additional candidates move from a nonideological "diverse" faction in 2019 and back into the more traditional community factions. The two candidates who switched factions were reported as having lost previous community endorsements over specific issues in local news at the time, and one was unable to obtain new endorsements and lost in his run for an eighth term, confirming that the observed switch is meaningful and not a mistake in the data. Candidates without factional support appear more willing to

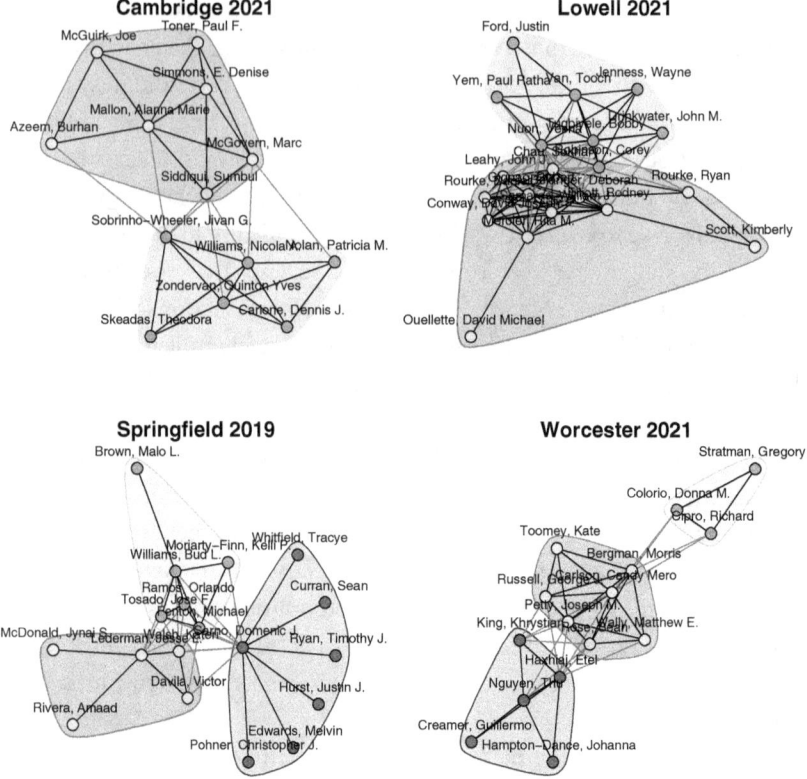

Figure 17 Sample Network Clusters, All Four Cities, Selected Years

run for open seats, as the proportion of isolated candidates is highest during the only year (2017) with more than one open seat. Contrary to some proponents' claims, we do not find evidence that donors spread out their money more in STV systems than plurality systems. One possible reason for this is that while Cambridge conducts nonpartisan city council elections, this does not restrict organizations from endorsing candidate slates, thus leading highly engaged donors to give primarily to candidates in one of two dominant emergent communities.

Figure 17 shows an example from 2021 of the two major candidate clusters in Lowell – one made up almost entirely of traditional white candidates and one including greater candidate diversity. While three clusters were identified in 2015 and 2017, this is somewhat misleading, as the third cluster is an artifact of a traditional core-periphery elite structure where core nodes are connected to one another but peripheral nodes are pendants only connected to core nodes and not each other (Borgatti and Everett 2000). Thus, nonincumbents who are not as well integrated into the political core of the city can serve as the basis for cluster definition (similar to what we find in all clusters in Springfield). This type of structure is distinct from a more traditional community – or factional – structure where the ties within a community are expected to be more dense than ties between two communities (Newman and Girvan 2004). Interestingly, the incumbents who belong to the peripheral cluster in 2015 appear to be somewhat out of step with the elite, as they all lost their seats by 2017.

The most interesting aspect of Lowell factions is the changing incorporation – or lack thereof – of more diverse candidates into the existing core-periphery structure. In all four cycles, there were between three and five Asian candidates, all of whom were of Cambodian descent. Although half were isolated in 2015, the Cambodian candidates comprised a large portion of the emergent diverse cluster in subsequent years. The sole exception belonging to the traditional faction is a successful Cambodian candidate, Sokhary Chau, who won with strong support from both traditional and diverse donor bases and was subsequently chosen as mayor. In 2021, the diverse faction also sponsored the first four Black candidates during the time period. Lowell politics appears to be in transition from a traditional core-periphery structure around a central political elite to a bi-factional party system, as it incorporates more diverse council members into the polity. Only time will tell whether or not the emergent progressive cluster supporting greater candidate diversity is incorporated into a transformed core-periphery structure, similar to Springfield, or if it develops a more distinctive platform beyond the initial push for racial diversity on the city council.

We identify three communities in each cycle for Springfield, as illustrated in the Springfield 2019 election pictured in Figure 17. However, this count is somewhat misleading, as Springfield upon closer inspection appears to have a traditional core-periphery structure of well-integrated incumbents surrounded by more peripheral candidates including "serious" nonincumbents backed by the establishment for open seats, and to a lesser extent incumbents not facing serious challenges. Thus, Figure 17 shows a tightly clustered core spread across the three communities that are defined by pendant nodes in each cluster. The outlying candidates who anchor the clusters are all either candidates for open seats (in all years except 2015), district incumbents, or very popular at-large incumbents (e.g., all clusters in 2015). Due to the prominent role of outlying nodes in community identification, candidates rarely belong to the same clusters from year to year and may even move from cluster to isolate (and back) depending on the perceived threat of the upcoming election. Although Springfield is more racially diverse than the other three cities, and the council composition ranges from fifty to sixty percent nonwhite, there is no indication that this diversity has solidified into factions within the city's political system. While there is a distinct two-person cluster of Hispanic candidates challenging (unsuccessfully) for an at-large seat in 2021, they are not linked to the two other Hispanic councilors who won ward elections. Thus, we conclude that Springfield is best described as a largely faction-less city with a traditional core-periphery structure, perhaps operating under regime politics (Stone 1989), at least for now.

The Worcester election shown in Figure 17 has three distinct clusters. As we shall demonstrate later in this section, in Figures 18 and 19, these clusters can be distinguished according to donor ideology. One cluster (in the upper right of the figure) consists of three candidates who identify as Republicans. This cluster appears in only two of the four election years we considered for Worcester. The two principal candidate clusters are more stable across elections: a more moderate cluster with a mix of at-large and incumbent ward candidates, and a more progressive cluster (lower left of the figure) featuring a higher proportion of candidates of color and from immigrant backgrounds, including a successful nonbinary candidate in 2021. Race can only partially explain the cleavage, as there are successful nonwhite candidates who are isolated or belong to the moderate cluster. Of the sixteen candidates who appear in at least two elections, only six switch between named clusters. Four are centrally located incumbents who arguably could belong to either faction, including long-time Mayor Joseph Petty and three district incumbents. The other two might be described as having been left behind by the growing diversity and progressiveness of the "new" progressive faction. Worcester, then, appears to be facing a potential transition to a local elite polarized around a mixture of race and ideology, although there are still strong signs of a more traditional core-periphery structure within the political elite.

We have two major findings from our initial analysis. First, there is a higher proportion of isolates in hybrid systems as compared to all at-large systems in Cambridge and Lowell, an issue we will return to in our discussion of election outcomes. Second, the four cities exhibit political cleavages that fall along a range of traditional core-periphery (Springfield) to fairly stable factions (Cambridge), with Lowell and Worcester in the midst of potential transitions from a traditional regime politics to more divisive ideological factions that are also split along racial lines. Donor patterns in Springfield suggest that racial diversity in and of itself is not a sufficient cause of a linear increase in factionalization, as the city now has a majority–minority council yet no indicators of race-based factionalization. Interestingly, the only potential impact of STV would be to increase factional structure in Cambridge, although we see no causal evidence that this is the case.

5.2 Donor Coalitions and Political Factions

We turn now to consideration of whether or not the characteristics of the coalition of donors giving to candidates within an identified political faction are distinct and stable across time. We link the donor-level data extracted from Catalist to the candidate factions identified in the previous section, and we estimate the average donor ideology and racial background (here, percent white) of these implicit donor coalitions. We include only donors contributing to candidates belonging to one of the identified network communities, and we exclude isolated candidates. If communities represent informal party networks, then we should expect to find differences in ideology between these communities. Given our earlier results, we might expect clear differences in Cambridge, some differences in Lowell and Worcester, and few if any differences in donor communities in Springfield. We might also find differences in the racial makeup of donors belonging to different communities, especially in Lowell where minority groups have staked major rights claims under the Voting Rights Act.

Figures 18 and 19 provide a summary of median donor ideology in each of the factions identified earlier over time. In Cambridge, although we identify stable candidate factions, the donors supporting them are not particularly distinctive in terms of ideology (Figure 18) or race (Figure 19). All of the donor clusters are extremely liberal, with average ideology scores of 70–85 (on a scale of 0–100). While the racial make-up of coalition donors varies from election to election, around ninety percent of donors to all coalitions are white, even the donors to the small (and nonpersistent) cluster of diverse candidates in 2019. While there may be ideological differences between the donor groups – as suggested by the clear difference in development proposals put forward by the respective community advocacy organizations – these differences are more specific to the locality and are not accurately measured on a national ideology scale.

Ironically, Figures 18 and 19 show that donors to Springfield's core/periphery clusters are less homogenous over time than those observed in Cambridge, although we expected to see similar donors across all clusters due to the regime politics at work in the city making candidate clusters

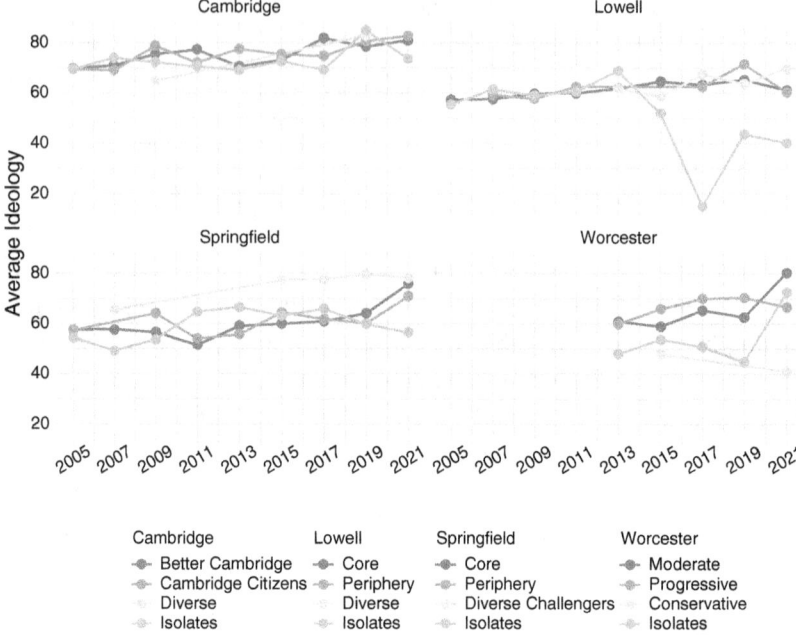

Figure 18 Average Donor Ideology in Each City Faction, Over Time

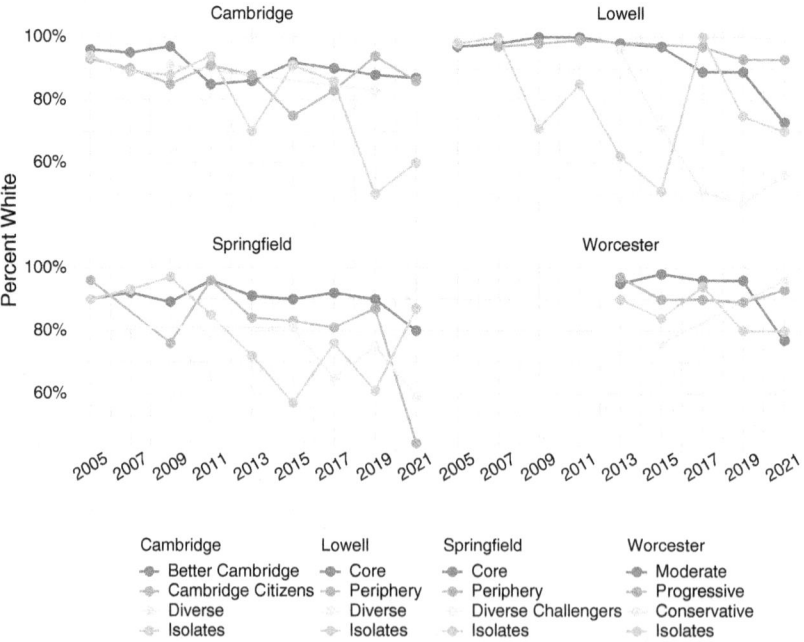

Figure 19 Proportion White Donors to Each City Faction, Over Time

highly unstable and sensitive to the particulars of a given election year. Our expectations for homogeneity are met in 2015 (with average ideology of sixty to seventy in all three clusters) and 2021 (average ideology of seventy to eighty in the two connected core clusters), but there is one more progressive peripheral cluster of nonincumbents in both 2017 and 2019 and the core donor base appears to move left during 2021. While it is difficult to confirm, we suspect that the apparent variation in cluster ideology is an artifact of election year variation in seat openings, taking into account the strong incumbent advantage observed in Springfield. District seat contestants may be well integrated into the core of citywide political elites but may otherwise draw from slightly different (and demographically distinct) donor bases at the district level. No district seats were open in 2015 (leading to a more conservative citywide donor base), while a mix of at-large and traditional minority district seats were open in 2017 and 2019, and only traditional minority district seats were open (or hotly contested) in 2021.

These figures show that racial, and to a lesser extent ideological, donor factions can be observed in Lowell. In contrast, Figures 18 and 19 show that divisions in Worcester are more ideological and less racial in character. In Lowell, the "Diverse" or "Progressive" donor coalition is around half white (range: forty-five to seventy-one percent white, with lower diversity later in the time series), while cluster ideology liberalizes over time moving from a fairly average of sixty in the first two elections to a slightly more progressive seventy (out of 100) in 2019 and 2021. The incumbent core (and peripheral core) clusters are overwhelmingly (around ninety-five percent) white prior to 2021, with consistent ideology scores in the low sixties. The higher proportion of nonwhite donors to candidates in the incumbent core in 2021 may indicate a growing incorporation of successful minority candidates into the traditional core-periphery structure. Worcester donor clusters fall almost entirely along ideological lines, and the gap between these two factions grows substantially over the four election cycles. While there is a significant nonwhite faction in 2015, it is also notably more conservative than the core incumbent (moderate) faction, and donors to a similar conservative faction in 2021 are not particularly racially diverse.

Overall, we find that the candidate factions identified earlier are distinct along racial and ideological lines, although the degree of distinctiveness depends more on whether a more factionalized local politics has replaced a traditional core-periphery structure than on the council structure or racial makeup of the city. Only Lowell has consistent factions over multiple years that vary significantly along racial lines. Worcester and Cambridge – two cities with a higher proportion of educated voters – have stable factions that vary along ideological lines, although only in Worcester are these ideological differences adequately captured by the national ideology scale.

5.3 Donor Networks in Elections

If the observed structure in candidate donor networks is an indicator of emergent factional politics at the local level, we would expect to see that candidates belonging to donor communities are more likely to be elected than those without organized political support, including not just donations but also endorsements and formal and informal campaign assistance. Table 5 summarizes the win rate of candidates depending on whether they belong to an identified cluster or are isolated within the donor network. Additionally, we test the significance

Table 5 Relationship between Donor Factions and Election Outcomes Network Communities and QAP Tests

City	Year	Community Winner Proportion	Isolate Winner Proportion	Test Value	Estimated p-value >=
Cambridge	2015	0.75	0	0.64	0.000
Cambridge	2017	0.69	0	0.53	0.000
Cambridge	2019	0.53	0	0.25	0.016
Cambridge	2021	0.69	0	0.28	0.014
Lowell	2015	0.69	0	0.65	0.000
Lowell	2017	0.50	0	0.27	0.021
Lowell	2019	0.53	0	0.45	0.002
Lowell	2021	0.48	0	0.13	0.140
Springfield	2015	0.91	0.19	0.51	0.000
Springfield	2017	0.82	0.31	0.23	0.035
Springfield	2019	0.60	0.36	0.15	0.099
Springfield	2021	0.60	0.50	0.07	0.266
Worcester	2015	0.67	0.27	0.21	0.047
Worcester	2017	1.00	0.17	0.50	0.000
Worcester	2019	0.80	0.33	0.24	0.056
Worcester	2021	0.67	0.33	0.27	0.023

of the relationship between donor network structure and winning an election using the quadratic assignment procedure (QAP) correlation test (Cranmer et al. 2017).[13] Overall, we find that nonincumbents in all systems *have almost no opportunity to win unless they belong to an organized donor community*, while incumbents in hybrid systems may continue to win even if they are less integrated into the core elite.

In Cambridge and Lowell, with only at-large elections, no isolated candidates win at-large seats. The relationship between community membership and winning in the hard-fought election in Lowell in 2021 (following the change to a hybrid city council system) is not quite significant, but this is likely because fewer than half of the candidates who belong to an organized community won a seat on the new council. Some of the district-level seats in Lowell may become safe for incumbents and allow them to change fundraising strategies, although the strong traces of emergent factionalization in the city suggest that this change is unlikely.

The hybrid systems in Springfield and Worcester allow some incumbent district candidates to win even without membership in one of the established donor factions. In both cities, isolated candidates are highly unlikely to be successful, particularly if they are nonincumbents. There is only one instance in each city where a nonincumbent manages to win as an isolated candidate, and neither exception undermines the general point. In 2015, Hispanic community organizer Adam Gomez won in Springfield as an isolated challenger running against an incumbent who was also isolated from the political elite. In 2019, conservative nonincumbent Donna Colorio won an at-large seat as an isolated candidate, but only while mounting a far more expensive simultaneous run for mayor.[14] Otherwise, the only candidates who win while isolated are long-standing incumbents, the majority of whom are district seat holders. This does not mean that running as an isolated candidate is a fool's errand in a city with a more unified political core. Springfield donors incorporate nonincumbents with widespread support into the political core, which helps decrease potential

---

[13] We create a matrix with the same dimensions as our donor networks, but rather than a tie indicating having donors in common, ties indicate winning one's election. That is, if candidate A and candidate B both win their election, we count a tie, and otherwise do not. We can then easily calculate the correlation between the two matrices. The QAP procedure is used to estimate a standard error by running simulations of network data (in our case, 1,000 times) that permute rows and columns in one matrix and measure a correlation coefficient of both matrices to produce an empirical distribution of correlations to which our observed correlation is compared.

[14] As we shall see in the next section, Colorio was also the beneficiary of a large amount of independent spending.

sources of factionalization, with five unsuccessful candidate isolates who performed comparatively well while losing later incorporated into one of the core donor clusters and in most cases winning a seat.

Overall, we find that candidates who are integrated into the donor community – both incumbents and nonincumbents – are more likely to win in all elections. As Table 5 shows, Quadratic Assignment Procedure (QAP) tests of this relationship yield significant results in twelve of sixteen elections. While total money raised might not be especially predictive of electoral success (see Section 3), having connections to other candidates via donors does correlate, more often than not, with election outcomes. Furthermore, the boost to election changes of shared donor networks appears particularly high when all members run at-large, whereas isolated candidates can win in hybrid systems.

5.4 Parties in Government?

Parties are, to be sure, much more than donor networks, with their basis in shared ideological or racial identities. Formal parties must build ideological orientations into shared platforms, and members of polarized parties rarely vote across party lines. If donor networks reflect informal parties in local government, then we might expect to find that votes on city ordinances would be structured by these emergent factions identified earlier. Specifically, are city council members more likely to vote similarly to the other candidates with whom they share donor support networks? As an initial investigation into this, we collected several nonunanimous city council votes for each city to see how these correlate with the donor networks we identified. These votes (described in greater detail in Online Appendix B) were chosen because they received significant local media coverage and can thus be regarded as among the most important council votes of these sessions. They are therefore not representative of all council votes, but are meant to demonstrate one way in which we might identify parties in government. They show that the outcomes of the council votes we described in the introductory pages of this Element reflect enduring factional conflicts.

Table 6 breaks down vote patterns for chosen votes by faction. If a faction votes as a bloc, we would expect to see either 100 percent (all in favor) or 0 percent (all opposed). If a faction splits its vote, we would see a vote proportion closer to fifty percent (half supporting and half opposing). While we can only investigate winning candidates, we use donor communities as identified in Figure 18. The analysis is made more complex by the

Table 6 City Council Vote Patterns, by Faction

Cambridge

Year	Issue	A Better Cambridge	Cambridge Residents	Cambridge Diverse	Final Vote
2017	Bicycle Safety Law	50% (4)	100% (5)	—	7-2
2019	Bicycle Safety Law	60% (5)	100% (3)	100% (1)	7-2
	Home Rule Petition	80% (5)	0% (3)	0% (1)	4-5
	Limit Developer Money	60% (5)	100% (3)	100% (1)	7-2
2021	Energy Use Disclosure – Healthcare Facilities	67% (6)	0% (3)	—	4-5
	Energy Use Disclosure – Large Apt Buildings	83% (6)	0% (3)	—	5-4
	Energy Use Disclosure Implementation Date	33% (6)	100% (3)	—	5-4

Lowell

Year	Issue	Incumbent Core	Incumbent Periphery	Diverse	Final Vote
2015	Ban Replica Guns	60% (5)	100% (3)	100% (1)	7-2
	Relocate New High School	40% (5)	100% (3)	0% (1)	5-4
2017	Mayor Selection	50% (6)	0% (1)	100% (2)	5-4
	Vice-Mayor Selection	83% (6)	0% (1)	100% (2)	7-2
2019	Declaring Racism a Public Health Crisis	29% (7)	—	100% (2)	4-5
	Direct Election of Mayor	86% (7)	—	0% (2)	6-3

(*Continued*)

Table 6 (Continued)

Springfield

Year	Issue	Core	Periphery 1/ Challengers	Periphery 2/ Diverse Challengers	Isolates	Final Vote
2015	Civilian Police Division	100% (5)	0% (3)	100% (2)	100% (3)	10-3
	Civilian Police Division (Veto Override)	100% (5)	0% (3)	50% (2)	100% (3)	9-4
2017	Declare Sanctuary City	75% (4)	100% (5)	0% (1)	66% (3)	10-3
2019	Civilian Police Division Lawsuit	75% (4)	67% (3)	100% (2)	100% (4)	11-2
	Police Budget Cuts (June 2020)	25% (4)	67% (3)	100% (2)	75% (4)	8-5
	Police Budget Cuts (June 2021)	25% (4)	0% (3)	0% (2)	25% (4)	2-11
2021*	City Budget (June 2022)	50% (4)	50% (2)	—	83% (6)	8-4
	Suspension of Trash Pickup Fee	75% (4)	100% (2)	—	33% (6)	7-5
	City Budget (June 2023)	50% (4)	100% (2)	—	83% (6)	10-2

Worcester

Year	Issue	Moderate	Progressive	Isolates and Conservative	Final Vote
2017	Support for City Busing	17% (6)	33% (3)	50% (2)	3-8
2019	Remove Christopher Columbus Statue	0% (5)	33% (3)	33% (3)	2-8
2021	Remove Christopher Columbus Statue	17% (6)	100% (3)	50% (2)	5-6
	Ban New Gas Stations	17% (6)	100% (3)	50% (2)	5-6
	Ban Crisis Pregnancy Centers	50% (6)	100% (3)	0% (2)	6-5
	Affirm Abortion Rights	50% (6)	100% (3)	50% (2)	7-4
	Inclusionary Zoning Law	0% (6)	100% (3)	50% (2)	4-7

Note: Percentages show proportion of faction voting yes. Total N in each faction shown in parentheses.
* Shortly after being reelected to office, Councilor Marcus Williams resigned from office resulting in only twelve councilors for this term.

existence of elected officials who were isolated from the identified donor communities, particularly in Springfield.

As expected, we find fairly clear evidence of party-style voting in Cambridge, with the "Cambridge Citizens" cluster voting in lockstep on all contentious votes included here, while the "A Better Cambridge" candidates often split, with the more centrist members joining the progressives to form a majority. A quick analysis of all contentious votes between 2020 and 2023 (available in online Appendix D) confirms this propensity for the progressive members to vote as a coalition, often joined by two to four more centrist council members. Also, as expected on the basis of earlier findings, we find little evidence of factional voting patterns in Springfield. While there may be some years in which a bloc of two or three council members act in unison, it is difficult to identify and if it does exist, there is little persistence in these ideological coalitions over time.

Perhaps surprisingly, given the less pronounced local factionalization, we find patterns of unified progressive voting in both Lowell and Worcester as well that are similar to those observed in Cambridge. These patterns reinforce the earlier observations that appeared consistent with the emergence of progressive factions in both cities over this time period. Council members elected as part of Lowell's "Diverse" faction, as well as those in the less stable "Peripheral" faction that appears to be somewhat more conservative, vote consistently with others in the coalition on the critical votes identified, with more centrist swing votes from the "Core" faction deciding the council outcomes. In Worcester, the majority of votes included are from the 2021 election cycle, with a strong and diverse progressive faction that clearly votes as a bloc joined by the more liberal isolates and members of the "Moderate" coalition.

5.5 Conclusions

This section has looked at the dynamics of informal party networks in four cities using a network analysis of donors shared amongst candidates. Using this approach, we find that there are distinct and consistent factions over time in each city, and that these factions represent stable and distinctive factions and pursue distinctive legislative agendas. Cambridge is perhaps the best example of a city with two long-standing and formalized political factions, although the donor base is fairly uniform according to national ideology scales. By contrast, the most racially diverse city we study, Springfield, is a classic example of a cohesive core political elite that incorporates rising political figures likely to win open seats regardless of race or background. Lowell and Worcester fall on the spectrum between, with long-standing moderate coalitions similar to those in Springfield facing new threats from increasingly cohesive emergent progressive coalitions that are distinctive in terms of both ideology and race.

In addition, we find that candidates in all cities who are integrated into a donor faction are more likely to be elected than those whose donor base is more isolated from core elites. That is, having ties to other candidates via donors is significantly correlated with electoral success. The extent of this advantage appears to depend on the type of city council system in use. All at-large city councils encourage candidates to work actively with the core political elite, while candidates in hybrid systems appear to have more latitude to run even while not actively courting donations from well-connected donors. This suggests that hybrid systems are more open to political newcomers.

6 Interest Groups

While direct donations from individuals are the most common way to fund a political campaign, another funding source is PAC donations. PACs pool money from individuals to then strategically distribute the funds to one or more candidates. Unions and business interests frequently use PACs to leverage members' contributions. Though PACs may conjure images of national and state elections, research has found that they appear in local politics, as well (Benjamin 2022).

Many studies of local elections have observed that business interests and labor unions play a major role in municipal elections. Anzia (2022), Adams (2010), Hartney (2022), and Krebs (2004) contend that groups such as teachers' unions, public employees' unions, real estate interests, and labor unions involved in construction tend to dominate local politics. These studies also emphasize the role that property developers play in supporting candidates, and they note that because municipal elections have such low turnout, local business interests tend to be particularly influential.

In this section, we address PAC activity in Cambridge, Lowell, Springfield, and Worcester. We ask how much PAC spending there is, how PACs distribute their money, whether PAC donations map onto the political factions we identified in Section 5, and whether there is a difference between PACs that give directly to candidates and those that engage in advocacy independently of candidates (so-called Super PACs). We find that PAC contributions across all four cities, like PAC contributions in congressional elections, play a significant role in candidate fundraising. The vast majority of PAC contributions come from groups backed by unions; in some cycles, unions comprise above ninety percent of all PAC contributions. Contrary to work focusing on the importance of public-sector unions, we find that the bulk of the union PAC contributions are typically from unions that primarily represent private-sector workers. In some cities in certain years, though, we do see notable instances where public-sector unions, such as teachers' unions, made large contributions in elections where there were relevant policy issues at stake.

One possible interpretation of this pattern is that public-sector unions may be able to mobilize voters through advertising, endorsements, or word of mouth, while craft unions may have a smaller public constituency to mobilize (Hartney 2022; Gaudette 2025). An assertion that a candidate is supported by teachers may influence the votes of the parents of school-age children, while a claim that a candidate will help plumbers or electricians may fall on deaf ears.

Other types of PACs play a much smaller role in contributing to candidates in the four cities. Issue-based and ideological PACs are largely absent from lists of contributors, but we do see significant issue group influence in Super PAC spending. We suspect that some business owners contribute as individuals, so a focus on PACs may underestimate business influence. Given the size of these cities, prominent business owners are likely known to the candidates, so the recipients of their contributions can observe the influence of their businesses even if it is difficult for researchers to measure this. It does seem evident, however, that (as is the case at the national level) wealthy individuals with strong ideological views find it more effective to influence elections through independent expenditures.

Finally, we find that PACs often participate in factional politics. In a number of years across each of the cities, PACs gave significantly more to one of the factions identified in Section 5. PACs' willingness to engage in factional politics seems to depend on the city, however, and in some years, they give more equitably across factions. Across all cities, PACs give most to incumbents, and when they give to nonincumbents, these nonincumbents usually win. These patterns mirror findings at the federal level (Open Secrets 2023). As we demonstrate in Section 5, candidates who are in network communities fare better electorally than those who are not; the fact that PACs focus their money on winning candidates suggests PACs give strategically, likely in order to increase access to public officials.

6.1 Coding PAC Contributions

Before 2021, Massachusetts did not require donations to be marked as from PACs on the state's disclosure forms. We therefore took the full set of donations from 2015 to 2021 and categorized as a PAC any donor name that included keywords commonly associated with PACs – for example, "committee," "association," and "Friends of." We then reviewed this list manually for errors, and hand-coded each PAC according to what type of constituency it served. We coded any PAC that represented a for-profit company interest as a business PAC. We coded as issue PACs any organizations whose name suggested that were incorporated to advance a policy interest. We coded as party PACs any PAC aligned with either the Democratic or Republican Party, whether they are state, town, or city campaign committees. PACs that are associated with a union and any coalition of union interests were coded as union PACs. We additionally hand-coded each union PAC as representing public employees if the union specifies that it primarily represents public governmental workers, teachers, firefighters, or police officers. Any union that primarily represents craft or service workers was coded as private. Some unions describe themselves as representing both public and private unions; for these unions, we classified them as having mixed membership. It is worth noting that union type may vary across locals. For example, the SEIU Local 888 represents public-sector workers, the SEIU 1199 represents private-sector workers, and the SEIU Local 509 highlights both its public- and private-sector workers. In cases in which the contribution record contains only a union with no information about the local, the union was coded as including the range of employees. In the case of an ambiguous SEIU entry, we coded it as mixed.

6.2 PAC Contributions across Our Four Cities

Table 7 shows the amounts contributed in each city by different types of groups over time. We can draw some general conclusions from these patterns, as well as some city-specific conclusions. Labor unions are consistently the dominant PAC contributors in all cities across all years. The unions that give are predominantly private craft unions; government employees such as teachers, firefighters, or the police are occasional participants but they play a much smaller role than previous literature might have predicted. Across each city we find that construction-related craft unions are quite active in their donations. While other work suggests public unions play a large role in local campaign finance (e.g., Anzia 2022), we find fairly

Table 7 Political Action Committee Contributions, All Four Cities, 2015–2021

Group Type	Union Type	Union Profession*	2015	2017	2019	2021
Cambridge						
$ Total			52,621	70,773	47,200	38,800
Union%			95.6	96.5	97.2	92.9
	Private		76.5	72.0	81.3	81.3
	Public		8.9	12.0	4.4	1.4
	Both		14.5	14.0	14.4	17.3
		Craft	71.0	69.6	75.4	63.5
		Mixed	14.5	14.1	15.3	24.3
		Gov't Worker	3.2	5.3	4.4	1.4
		Transportation	3.6	1.7	2.8	6.7
Business%			1.4	0.6	2.1	1.9
Issue%			2.1	2.2	0.5	5.2
Party%			1.0	0.7	0.0	0.0
Lowell						
$ Total			21,854	21,050	173,060	39,900
Union%			67.0	95.3	64.0	100
	Private		54.0	31.0	69.0	57.0
	Public		21.0	33.0	18.0	28.0
	Both		25.0	36.0	13.0	15.0

(Continued)

Table 7 (Continued)

Group Type	Union Type	Union Profession*	2015	2017	2019	2021
		Craft		54.0	31.2	62.6
		Mixed		25.0	36.2	12.5
		Firefighters		10.0	9.0	3.7
		Teachers		11.0	16.2	5.0
		Gov't Worker		0.0	7.5	7.5
Business%			0.0	2.4	0.9	0.0
Issue%			0.0	1.0	0.2	0.0
Party%			33.0	1.4	34.9	0.0
Springfield						
$ Total			41,857	57,969	45,065	25,525
Union%			90.0	91.4	90.5	96.1
	Private		58.0	59.0	54.0	50.7
	Public		9.7	11.0	15.0	9.8
	Both		32.3	30.0	31.0	39.6
		Craft	45.9	37.7	41.9	27.2
		Mixed	25.2	20.5	17.8	29.4
		Police	5.5	3.3	2.9	0.8
		Service Workers	5.9	10.3	13.2	11.2
		Healthcare	13.3	20.3	12.3	22.4
		Firefighters	2.3	4.3	7.8	9.0
		Teachers				53.5
						15.3
						4.0
						11.9
						5.0

Business%			3.1		5.9		6.5	0.0
Issue%			6.2		2.7		1.6	3.1
Party%			0.7		0.0		1.3	0.8

Worcester

$ Total			52,342		55,929		58,300	66,135
Union%			77.8		86.0		98.3	95.3
	Private		58.0	67.4		65.0		69.5
	Public		14.0	8.3		11.0		2.9
	Both		27.0	24.3		24.0		27.6
		Craft	49.5	55.5		60.6		62.2
		Mixed	26.0	23.1		24.0		27.6
		Firefighters	8.2	4.5		9.9		0.4
		Healthcare	5.3	5.5		0.2		4.0
		Transportation	2.9	5.9		4.5		3.1
Business%			1.5	2.3		0.9		0.0
Issue%			14.1	9.7		0.0		0.6
Party%			6.6	2.0		0.9		4.1

* Union Profession percentages only include professions that contributed five percent in one or more city election cycles; totals in this category do not sum to 100.

consistent evidence to the contrary. One reason we find different results may be due to case selection – slight variation in a city's union density could lead to significant differences in campaign giving. Another reason may be due to strategies used by public-sector unions. We do not consider in-kind donations, nor do we consider the role of endorsements, both of which could be powerful tools of public-sector unions (Gaudette 2025). Public-sector unions, like teachers' unions, also have significant access to a large group of constituents: parents. So, as the scope of the types of cities studied by scholars of urban affairs, we may find more evidence of idiosyncratic strategies by unions depending on who they represent and the context of their city. Some unions, and some nonunion groups, play idiosyncratic roles reflecting either short-term issues and candidacy decisions (as is the case for the explosion of donations in Lowell in 2019) or distinctive economic concerns of these cities (as is the case for the role played by healthcare and service workers in Springfield). In contrast to the other cities, we see a notable amount of donations from issue-based PACs in Worcester, particularly in years where we saw in Section 5 that the Republican candidate faction was stronger.

6.3 PAC Factionalism

In the previous section, we examined candidates' shared networks of individual donors and identified party factions. These factions represent either divergent ideological agendas on municipal issues or racial/ethnic cleavages. Individuals who contribute to multiple candidates in a faction, while not contributing to the other side, are either plugged into the municipal political scene and want to advance one of the factions, or are mobilized by multiple candidates in the faction to participate. Here we ask whether PACs support one side of the political factions that were identified, or whether they strategically donate, contributing to candidates in multiple factions to ensure access regardless of who wins. We mapped PAC contributions onto the individual donor networks, calculating the total amount donated by PACs in each city to candidates in each faction. Where applicable, we note whether the contributions were given to candidates in the core of a faction, on the periphery, or on candidates that were completely removed from donor networks (isolates). These results are shown in Figure 20. A full narrative of PAC activities in provided in Online Appendix C.

In Cambridge, PAC contributions primarily went to candidates affiliated with A Better Cambridge. Only in 2015 did candidates not slated by

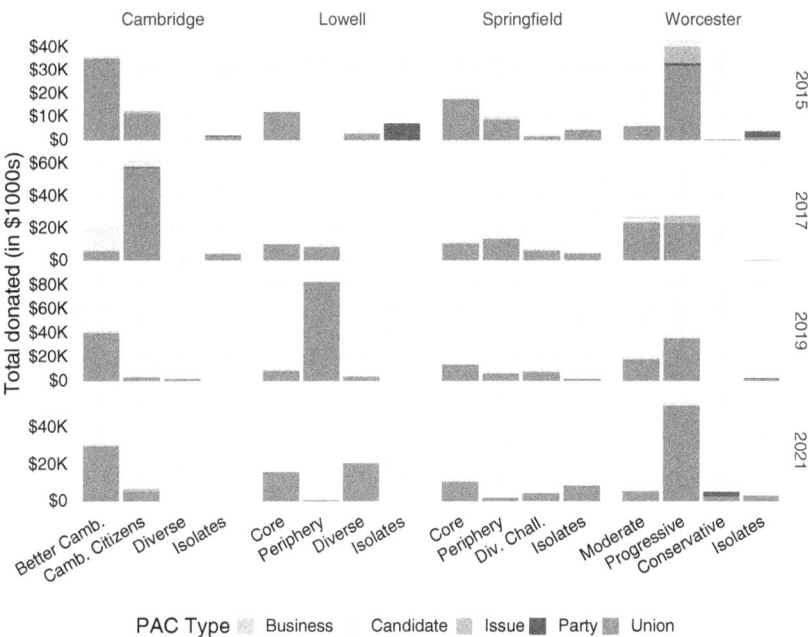

Figure 20 PAC Contributions by Network Community, PAC Type, and City, 2015–2021

this group receive notable PAC support. As would be expected in an STV system where candidates receive endorsements that effectively group them into slates, there were very few contributions to candidates not in a faction. The slating groups themselves, however, did not give directly to candidates; some of them made independent expenditures on behalf of their full slate (as described in the next section of this section).

For the 2015 and 2017 cycles, PAC donations in Lowell mirror those in Cambridge. These groups contributed exclusively to the network core and periphery, with no donations being sent to the diverse faction. The situation changed dramatically in 2019, however. While the core network still received a substantial amount of PAC donations in 2019, the diverse network received approximately four times as much money from PACs. And in 2021, the two factions received equal amounts of contributions.

In Springfield, as would be expected from a more machine-like political system, PACs behave similarly to individual donors. Most donations are concentrated among the core-periphery structure, including well-integrated incumbents and "serious" nonincumbents backed by the establishment for open seats. There are also more pronounced contributions to candidates not connected to the political network (isolates), which is consistent with the fact that there are a number of incumbents receiving PAC money who do not face serious challenges.

PACs in Worcester split their donations across the moderate and progressive factions in the 2015 and 2017 cycles. Beginning in 2019, the moderate faction starts receiving notably more money from PACs, and in 2021, PAC contributions to the moderate faction dwarf the money going to the progressive faction. It is noteworthy that conservative candidates receive almost no PAC money in Worcester, and, after 2015, there is virtually no money going to candidates outside of the informal party structures.

We saw in Section 3 (Figures 2 and 4) that PACs overwhelmingly favor incumbents across all four cities. In Cambridge, for example, there are almost no PAC contributions to nonincumbents in three of the election cycles we considered. And while there was substantial PAC support for nonincumbents in Worcester in 2015, these contributions declined in each subsequent election cycle. These data strongly suggest that PACs are most electorally active in supporting candidates who are already in office and who have shown they are friendly to their interests. Given that union PACs are the most prominent contributors, these incumbent lawmakers are most likely to be labor aligned.

In Figure 21, we show that the vast majority of candidates that receive PAC money win their elections. Incumbents who receive PAC contributions are especially likely to be reelected. Of course, given that incumbents on the local level are reelected at high rates (Oliver 2012), this is unsurprising. But we also find that PACs consistently fund nonincumbents that ultimately win. We see this most clearly in the two cases where there was the largest PAC spending on nonincumbents: Worcester in 2015 and Lowell in 2019. In both cases, PACs made substantial donations to victorious nonincumbents (in the diverse Lowell faction, and across the moderate and progressive faction in Worcester). Only in Cambridge did PACs contribute to nonincumbents aligned with an existing network that ultimately lost. The success of PAC-backed nonincumbents illuminates the dominance of incumbents in Figure 2, and why spikes in donations to nonincumbents are followed by years with greater proportions of incumbent donations – PACs support nonincumbents who win reelection and continue to receive PAC spending in future cycles.

6.4 Independent Expenditures

After the U.S. Supreme Court's landmark decision in *Citizens United v. FEC* and the subsequent Appellate Court ruling in *SpeechNow.org v. FEC*, there has been a rise in "Super PACs," PACs that exclusively

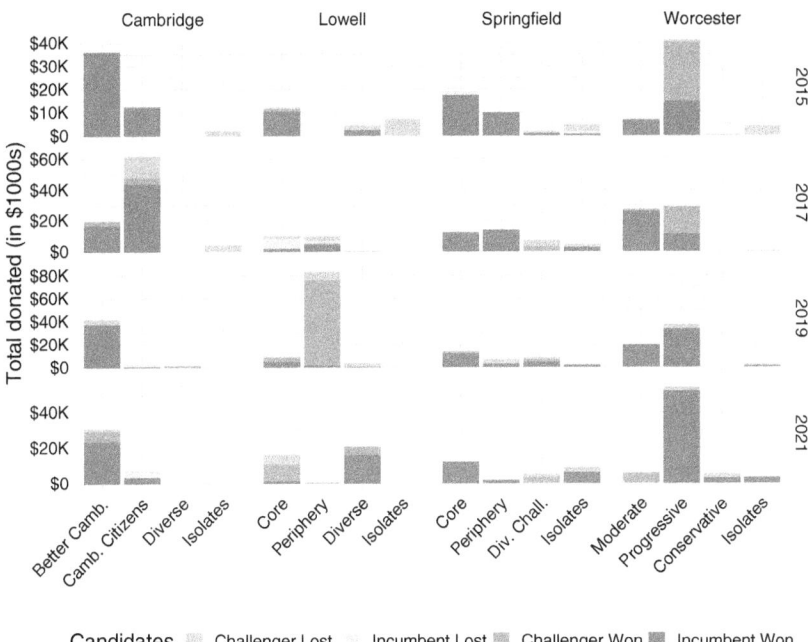

Figure 21 PAC Contributions by Network Community, Election Result, and City, 2015–2021

spend money independently of political candidates. While much work has been done to track independent expenditure PACs in federal and state elections, there has been little work on how these entities behave on the local level. How much independent PAC spending do we see in these mid-size municipalities, and how are these PACs different from PACs that contribute directly to candidates?

Table 8 shows all independent expenditures in the four cities we looked at for the 2013 to 2021 election cycles. Independent expenditures increased substantially over this time period, but they increased in different ways in the four cities. In three of these cities (Lowell, Worcester, and Springfield), independent expenditure groups are not consistently active, but when they are, their expenditures far exceed PAC contributions.

Independent expenditure groups play the largest role in Cambridge. Four organizations that raise money mostly from Cambridge citizens used the money to engage in advocacy for candidate slates, distributing palm cards and other material listing endorsements. This is almost certainly a consequence of Cambridge's adaptation to STV. The groups that spend large sums of money use these expenditures to communicate to the public

Table 8 Independent Expenditures, All Four Cities, 2015–2021

Cycle	City	Amount	Group	Recipients	Donors
2017	Cambridge	1,792	Cambridge Bicycle Safety IE PAC	Multiple	Multiple
2019	Cambridge	3,285	Cambridge Bicycle Safety IE PAC	Multiple	Multiple
2021	Cambridge	11,178	A Better Cambridge IE PAC	Multiple	Multiple
2021	Cambridge	23,353	Cambridge Citizens Coalition IE PAC	Multiple	Multiple
2021	Cambridge	1,500	Priorities for Progress IE PAC	One candidate	Multiple
2019	Lowell	49,897	Building a Stronger Commonwealth	Multiple	IUPAT
2021	Multiple, Including Springfield	17,000	Environmental League of Massachusetts Action Fund IE PAC	Multiple	Multiple
2019	Multiple, Including Worcester	267,429	Massachusetts Majority IE PAC	Multiple	Multiple
2021	Multiple, Including Worcester	258,937	Massachusetts Majority IE PAC	Multiple	Multiple
2015	Worcester	625	Retired Public Employees PAC	One candidate	Multiple
2021	Worcester	9,316	Worcester Working Families IE PAC	Multiple	Multiple
	Total	644,314			

about which slates of candidates they support and to explain how they wish voters to fill out their ranked ballots.

Other cities have similar organizations; for instance, a group was formed in Worcester in 2021 to advocate for a slate of progressive candidates. In Lowell, a city-specific organization funded almost entirely by the Painters' Union (IUPAT) engaged in advocacy for a slate of candidates in the 2019 election. In neither city are these groups consistent participants in elections.

Three statewide groups endorsed some candidates in these cities as part of a larger effort. These groups were not required to itemize spending per candidate. Among them were the Environmental League of Massachusetts, a 501(c)(4) group that spent on behalf of many municipal and state legislative candidates throughout the state over this time period, including two council candidates in Springfield, and the Massachusetts Majority PAC, a super PAC established by former Republican Governor Charlie Baker to support Republican candidates in municipal elections (Murphy 2019; McNamara 2023).

One of the biggest takeaways from Table 8 is that, in contrast to the direct PAC donations, there are more issue-based PACs among independent spenders. Unions occasionally play a role in independent expenditure campaigns, but for the most part, independent expenditure groups appear to be an outlet for individual donors who want to advocate for particular issues. As is the case in state and federal politics, contribution limits for direct contributions ensure that a donor who wishes to draw attention to a particular issue is unlikely to get his or her message across by contributing to candidates. This is particularly the case for at-large municipal elections, where it is difficult for issue appeals to influence election results. In Cambridge, the wealthiest of the four cities, there is a long history of slating organizations engaging in advocacy, and independent expenditure groups are a natural extension of that and of the STV system. In the less wealthy cities, occasional decisions by independent expenditure groups or donors to them can draw attention to the concerns of business leaders, activists, or party leaders, but they are not a regular occurrence.

6.5 Summary

Our data show that there is a robust level of PAC spending across all four cities in the time period we examine, although the total amount spent is significantly less than that contributed by individual donors and fluctuates by city across cycles. The most significant source of PAC money is unions, which are often responsible for over ninety percent of all PAC contributions. Private unions are consistently the biggest donors, fueled by those that represent craft workers, such as carpenters and electrical workers. Each of the four cities has some unique spending patterns reflecting its demographic and economic characteristics. In cities with a pattern of factional politics, such as Cambridge, Worcester, and Lowell, PACs may choose to either primarily fund one side or contribute across divides.

This choice may be consistent in a city or it may vary across cycles. PACs tend to support incumbents, but when they select nonincumbents, these nonincumbents often win.

The story we tell here, then, concerns access and influence. Groups that desire access give money to candidates; these groups tend to be labor unions that play a consistent role in city politics but do not have a significant ability to appeal to the public. Groups that wish to shape public attitudes are more likely to engage in independent expenditure campaigns. The nature of these groups varies across cities and over time, but it is driven by time-worn theories of interest group decision-making.

In closing, however, we emphasize again that our results here do not show that wealthy interests, be they businesses, property developers, local chambers of commerce, and so forth, do not shape local politics. Although we cannot prove this using the campaign finance data we have, it does seem evident that many individual donors do speak for these interests and that candidates and elected officials know this. Survey-based research and analyses of municipal spending decisions (e.g., Kaufmann 2004; Trounstine 2008; Hajnal 2009; Benjamin 2022) show this to be the case. Our results suggest, instead, that business interests choose not to contribute through PACs or to consistently engage in independent expenditure campaigns. They may not need to.

7 Conclusions and Implications

This Element has examined the politics of midsize American cities through the lens of campaign finance by analyzing candidate fundraising and donor networks. Our approach leverages a novel method to study local politics, addressing the challenges posed by limited and fragmented data that have traditionally hindered systematic analysis of municipal elections (Trounstine 2010; Einstein and Kogan 2016; Anzia 2022). In doing so, we aim to contribute to the broader understanding of how money and political influence operate below the state and federal levels, where much of the extant campaign finance literature has focused.

Candidates: In federal and state elections, rising advertising costs, intensifying partisanship, and shifts in legal regimes have produced a high-spending, polarized campaign environment (e.g., Drutman 2015; Barber 2016). By contrast, midsize municipal elections operate on a smaller scale. Candidates rarely need to advertise on television, and many are known personally in their communities. The officially nonpartisan nature of these contests, combined with low turnout and less media coverage, further reduces the role of money in shaping vote outcomes (Schaffner, Streb, and Wright 2001; Darr, Hitt, and Dunway 2021). In our study, we find that incumbents benefit from stable donor support, while nonincumbents struggle to compete unless they tap into new or outside sources of money. These dynamics mirror previous findings that municipal electoral institutions often discourage turnover and preserve political hierarchies (e.g., Hajnal and Trounstine 2005; Trounstine 2008; Anzia 2014, 2022; Einstein and Glick 2018).

We also find that changes to electoral rules – such as moving from at-large to district-based representation – can temporarily disrupt campaign finance patterns but do not result in lasting shifts in voter behavior or political spending. The use of the single transferable vote (STV), as in Cambridge, appears to increase total fundraising, but does so by encouraging coordinated slates and reinforcing ideological factions. This finding aligns with prior work showing that electoral rules can shape elite competition more than mass participation (Trounstine and Valdini 2008; Tausanovitch and Warshaw 2014). Our focus on midsize cities, where over a quarter of Americans reside, adds to a relatively thin empirical base and helps build generalizable knowledge about how urban political systems function outside of major metropolitan hubs.

Donors: Our analysis reveals that the donor pool in these cities remains remarkably stable over time in terms of donation size and general demographics. The share of very small donations has grown slightly, likely due to platforms like ActBlue lowering the transaction costs of participation. Perhaps more notable is the increased participation of women, who are becoming a larger share of donors, consistent with state and national trends (Schlozman, Verba, and Brady 2012; Albert and La Raja 2026). Yet, despite these modest shifts, the donor class in our cities remains predominantly white, affluent, and liberal – especially in Massachusetts, a context that tilts heavily Democratic.

We also find evidence of growing racial diversity in donor participation, particularly in Lowell, where Asian American giving has increased dramatically since the adoption of district-based elections. While Springfield has seen some growth in Black donor participation, Hispanic residents remain underrepresented in all four cities. These findings echo work by Benjamin (2017) and Schiff (2022), which highlights how race, geography, and political opportunity structure engagement. We also find that zip code-based analyses of donor income are more limited in midsize cities, which often contain only a handful of zip codes, limiting spatial resolution compared to studies in large metropolitan areas.

Parties: Although municipal elections are officially nonpartisan, we find strong evidence of informal party-like behavior through campaign donor networks. These networks are not only stable over time but also distinguishable by ideology and race. Candidates with strong network connections – especially those sharing donors with past winners – are more likely to succeed. These findings reinforce arguments by Hopkins (2018) and de Benedictis-Kessner and Warshaw (2016) about the nationalization of local elections and the role of partisan identity in shaping political competition. Our analysis adds to this literature by showing that donor networks operate as de facto political organizations, not only structuring competition but also providing cues for voters in low-information environments.

However, the link between donor networks and policy outcomes remains ambiguous. In some cases – particularly around polarizing issues such as climate policy or reproductive rights – we see alignment between donor clusters and city council votes. In other cases, city politics appears to be more idiosyncratic or driven by interpersonal relationships, especially in cities with lower levels of ideological polarization. This echoes findings by Oliver, Ha, and Callen (2012) that individual familiarity can override broader partisan signals in small-scale political environments.

Interest Groups: We also document the growing influence of PACs and independent expenditures (IEs) in local politics. PAC contributions are still dwarfed by individual giving in aggregate, but PACs – especially from private-sector unions – make much larger average donations. These unions play a more active role in midsize cities than public-sector unions, which tend to engage selectively when institutional stakes are high (Anzia 2022). Business PACs remain less active, although issue PACs often shape the independent expenditure landscape. IEs in Cambridge, in particular, have been used strategically to support slates under the STV system, further reinforcing elite control.

Overall, PACs and IEs contribute to the factional dynamics we identify in donor networks, with their support often tilted toward incumbents or aligned factions. When PACs back nonincumbents, those candidates tend to win – suggesting that strategic PAC engagement can be decisive, especially when party infrastructure is weak. These findings build on research at the national level showing that interest groups increasingly operate outside traditional party systems to shape policy agendas (Drutman 2015).

In short, this Element offers a comprehensive look at how campaign finance structures and reveals the contours of municipal politics in midsize American cities. We show how donor networks substitute for party organizations, how race and ideology shape donor coalitions, and how campaign finance interacts with electoral and institutional structures. These findings expand on recent work emphasizing the reproduction of political inequality at the local level and offer a framework for future research on how elites, institutions, and networks shape local democratic representation.

7.1 Implications for Political Reform

We can draw several key implications about influence and inequality in campaign finance within midsize cities. Despite their smaller scale, these elections reproduce patterns of unequal political engagement common at the state and federal levels. Incumbents and well-connected candidates benefit from stable donor networks, which limit opportunities for grassroots challengers. Although some cities have made progress in diversifying their donor bases, white and affluent communities continue to dominate campaign giving, skewing representation and policy responsiveness toward the interests of a narrow segment of the population (Gilens 2012; Schlozman, Verba, and Brady 2012).

Nonpartisan municipal elections often reinforce these dynamics. Donor networks function as informal party-like structures that recruit and sustain candidates. Because these structures are opaque, voters often lack cues about candidate affiliations or policy alignments. In some cities, dominant donor coalitions operate like political monopolies, reducing competition and weakening democratic accountability (Trounstine 2008).

Reforms to electoral rules may help mitigate these issues. In Lowell, district-based elections have improved minority representation, yet in other cities, campaign finance remains heavily skewed toward older, wealthier, and ideologically liberal donors – many of whom differ substantially from the broader electorate. These imbalances are amplified by low turnout, which favors wealthier and more educated voters with more ideological views (Hajnal and Trounstine 2005; Anzia 2014).

RCV, while intended to reduce conflict and broaden participation, may not deliver such results in practice. In Cambridge, the use of STV has led to factionalized fundraising, as donors concentrate resources on slates of aligned candidates. Issue-based PACs – especially union-backed ones – have become major players in independent expenditures, funding campaigns around housing, environmental, and labor priorities. These trends reflect broader national patterns where independent expenditures skew policy in favor of well-organized groups with resources (Anzia 2014; Hertel-Fernandez 2018).

To address these inequities, several reforms could enhance fairness and representation. Increasing voter turnout remains the most effective strategy. Aligning municipal elections with federal and state cycles, expanding early voting, and targeting registration in underrepresented communities would engage a broader electorate (Browning, Marshall, and Tabb 2003). Public financing programs, such as New York City's matching system, might reduce reliance on habitual donors and attract a broader set of contributors within the city.

Finally, supporting candidates from low-income and minority backgrounds could improve descriptive and substantive representation. Local governments and civic groups should offer candidate training and encourage community-based fundraising. These steps would help reduce barriers for first-time candidates and create alternatives to entrenched donor networks. Addressing the financial burden of holding office – through stipends or other support – would also make public service more accessible (Straus 2025).

7.2 The Value of Our Approach for Studying Local Politics

We believe that highlighting our methodical contribution for studying local politics will help advance new research. Our study employs a unique dataset that merges campaign finance records with voter demographic information, providing an unprecedented level of detail about municipal elections. Unlike many prior studies that focus on large cities, this analysis has captured patterns in midsize cities, where local politics often functions differently but remains underexplored. The use of Massachusetts' standardized campaign finance reporting system ensures a high-quality, comparable dataset across multiple election cycles, avoiding many of the data inconsistencies that plague municipal election studies in other states. By integrating Catalist voter file data, the study provides detailed insights into the race, age, income, and ideology of donors. These data allow for a richer understanding of who funds local campaigns and why than has previously been possible. Our work exploits a networks approach to revealing political factions in nonpartisan elections, examining the ideological and racial bases of these latent cleavages.

The study's longitudinal approach, spanning over eighteen years across four cities, enables an analysis of campaign finance trends over time, rather than relying on single-election snapshots. This makes it possible to evaluate how changes in election systems, demographics, and political dynamics may influence campaign financing over time. Moreover, the study bridges gaps in existing research, which has largely focused either on large cities or survey data. By focusing on midsize cities, this study highlights unique patterns in local elections that might be obscured in broader analyses, such as the role of informal party factions in nonpartisan elections, the persistent advantage of incumbents in low-turnout races, and the relatively low engagement of interest groups in local finance compared to state and federal elections.

Despite its strengths, the study could be expanded in several ways. First, while Massachusetts' standardized reporting system provides high-quality data, the study remains geographically limited, focusing only on one state. Expanding the analysis to midsize cities in other states with different political cultures and campaign finance laws would improve generalizability. Future research could include cities with more competitive partisan environments or different regulatory frameworks to assess whether the findings hold across a broader sample.

Second, the study relies on financial contributions as the primary measure of political influence, but money is not the only factor shaping local elections. Incorporating qualitative data from interviews with candidates, donors, and campaign strategists could help uncover why donors choose specific candidates, how candidates target different funding sources, and how local political elites perceive financial power in municipal elections. Additionally, surveying small-dollar donors could provide insights into their motivations and whether public financing reforms might encourage broader participation. The study could also explore alternative measures of political influence beyond campaign finance, such as endorsement networks, local media coverage, and social media mobilization. As seen in the Worcester bike lane controversy, grassroots activism and social media outrage can sometimes shape policy more than financial contributions. Future research could examine whether major donors also serve as local political influencers in other ways, such as organizing events, mobilizing voters, or shaping public discourse.

Third, while the study tracks independent expenditures and PAC donations, a deeper dive into the strategies of interest groups could be beneficial. The study notes that interest groups play a relatively small role in direct financing but can still shape policy agendas through targeted independent expenditures. A more systematic analysis of which interest groups engage in local races, what issues drive their spending, and how their influence compares to individual donors and informal party networks would add depth to the findings.

In sum, we have sought in this study to make a significant contribution by using innovative data analysis methods to uncover the dynamics of campaign finance in midsize cities, a crucial but understudied area of American politics. Our combination of campaign finance records, voter demographic data, and comparative city analysis provides new insights into how money interacts with local political structures, incumbency advantages, and factional competition. However, expanding the geographic scope, integrating qualitative data, examining nonfinancial influence mechanisms, and further analyzing interest group behavior would enhance the study's impact and applicability. By addressing these areas, future research could provide an even clearer picture of the intersection between money, partisanship, power, and local democracy.

Bibliography

Abrams, Richard M. 1964. *Conservatism in a Progressive Era: Massachusetts Politics, 1900–1912*. Cambridge, MA: Harvard University Press.

Adams, Brian, and Ping Ren. 2006. "Asian Americans and Campaign Finance in Municipal Elections." *Social Science Journal* 43 (3): 597–615.

Adams, Brian. 2010. *Campaign Finance in Local Elections: Buying the Grassroots*. Boulder, CO: First Forum Press/Lynne Reinner Publishers.

Adams, Brian. 2011. "Financing Local Elections: The Impact of Institutions on Electoral Outcomes and Democratic Representation." *Political Science* 44 (1): 111–112.

Albert, Zachary, and Raymond J. La Raja. 2026. *Small Donors in American Politics: Myth and Reality*. Chicago: University of Chicago Press.

Aldrich, John H. 1995. *Why Parties? The Origin and Transformation of Political Parties in America*. Chicago: University of Chicago Press.

Amy, Douglas. 2002. *Real Choices, New Voices*. New York: Columbia University Press.

Anzia, Sarah F. 2014. *Timing and Turnout*. Chicago: University of Chicago Press.

Anzia, Sarah F. 2022. *Local Interests: Politics, Policy, and Interest Groups in U.S. City Governments*. Chicago: University of Chicago Press.

Arrington, Theodore S., and Gerald L. Ingalls. 1984. "Race and Campaign Finance in Charlotte, NC." *Western Political Quarterly* 37 (4): 578–583.

Austin, Sam, and Lisa Young. 2006. *Political Finance in City Elections: Toronto and Calgary Compared*. Calgary, AB: Institute for Advanced Policy Research, the University of Calgary.

Bachrach, Peter, and Morton S. Baratz. 1962. "Two Faces of Power." *American Political Science Review* 56 (4): 947–952.

Barber, Kathleen L. 1995. *Proportional Representation and Election Reform in Ohio*. Columbus: Ohio State University Press.

Barber, Kathleen L. 2000. *A Right to Representation: Proportional Election Systems for the Twenty-First Century*. Columbus: Ohio State University Press.

Barber, Michael J. 2016. "Representing the Preferences of Donors, Partisans, and Voters in the US Senate." *Public Opinion Quarterly* 80 (1): 225–249.

Bass, Adam. 2024. "Worcester Mill Street Redesign Hotly Contested as Crash Data Released." MassLive, May 24. www.masslive.com/

worcester/2024/05/worcester-mill-street-redesign-hotly-contested-as-crash-data-released.html.

Bawn, Katherine, Martin Cohen, David Karol, Seth Masket, Hans Noel, and John Zaller. 2012. "A Theory of Political Parties: Groups, Policy Demands and Nominations in American Politics." *Perspectives on Politics* 10 (3): 571–597.

Behr, Joshua G. 2004. *Race, Ethnicity, and the Politics of City Redistricting*. Albany: State University of New York Press.

Benjamin, Andrea. 2017. *Racial Coalition Building in Local Elections: Elite Cues and Cross-Ethnic Voting*. New York: Cambridge University Press.

Benjamin, Andrea, and Alexis Miller. 2019. "Picking Winners: How Political Organizations Influence Local Elections." *Urban Affairs Review* 55 (3): 643–674.

Benjamin, Andrea. 2022. "PACs Rule Everything around Me: How Political Action Committees Shape Elections and Policy in the Local Context." *Interest Groups & Advocacy* 11 (2): 278–302.

Borgatti, Stephen P., and Martin G. Everett. 2000. "Models of Core/periphery Structures." *Social Networks* 21 (4): 375–395.

Browning, Rufus, Dale Rogers Marshall, and David H. Tabb. 2003. *Racial Politics in American Cities*. New York: Longman.

Burnett, Craig M. 2018. "Parties as an Organizational Force on Nonpartisan City Councils." *Party Politics* 25 (4): 594–608.

Canon, David T. 1993. "Sacrificial Lambs or Strategic Politicians? Political Amateurs in U.S. House Elections." *American Journal of Political Science* 37 (4): 1119–1141.

Cho, Wendy K. Tam. 2001. "Foreshadowing Strategic Pan-Ethnic Politics: Asian American Campaign Finance Activity in Varying Multiethnic Contexts." *State Politics and Policy Quarterly* 1 (3): 273–294.

Cho, Wendy K. Tam. 2002. "Tapping Motives and Dynamics Behind Campaign Contributions: Insights from the Asian America Case." *American Politics Research* 30 (4): 347–383.

Clarke, Susan E. 1998. *The Work of Cities*. Minneapolis: University of Minnesota Press.

Cohan, Alexi. 2024. "The Rising Power of Women in Massachusetts Politics." WGBH, October 8. www.wgbh.org/news/politics/2024-10-08/the-rising-power-of-women-in-massachusetts-politics.

Collingwood, Loren, and Sean Long. 2021. "Can States Promote Minority Representation? Assessing the Effects of the California Voting Rights Act." *Urban Affairs Review* 57 (3): 731–762.

Cranmer, Skyler J., Philip Leifeld, Scott D. McClurg, and Meredith Rolfe. 2017. "Navigating the Range of Statistical Tools for Inferential Network Analysis." *American Journal of Political Science* 61 (1): 237–251.

Dahl, Robert A. 1961. *Who Governs? Democracy and Power in an American City*. New Haven, CT: Yale University Press.

Darr, Joshu P., Matthew P. Hitt, and Johanna L. Dunway. 2021. *Home Style Opinion: How Local Newspapers can Slow Polarization*. New York: Cambridge University Press, Elements in Politics and Communication.

de Benedictis-Kessner, Justin, and Christopher Warshaw. 2016. "Mayoral Partisanship and Municipal Fiscal Policy." *The Journal of Politics* 78 (4): 1124–1138.

de Benedictis-Kessner, Justin. 2018. "Off-Cycle and Off-Center: Election Timing and Representation in Municipal Government." *American Political Science Review* 112 (2): 261–273.

de Benedictis-Kessner, Justin, Diana Da In Lee, Yamil R. Velez, and Christopher Warshaw. 2023. "American Local Government Elections Database." *Scientific Data* 10: 912. https:doi.org/10.1038/s41597-023-02792.

de Benedictis-Kessner, Justin, Daniel Jones, and Christopher Warshaw. 2025. "How Partisanship in Cities Influences Housing Policy." *American Journal of Political Science* 69 (1): 64–77.

Desmarais, Bruce A., Raymond J. La Raja, and Michael S. Kowal. 2015. "The Fates of Challengers in U.S. House Elections: The Role of Extended Party Networks in Supporting Candidates and Shaping Electoral Outcomes." *American Journal of Political Science* 59 (1): 194–211.

Donovan, Todd, Caroline J. Tolbert, and Kellen Gracey. 2016. "Campaign Civility under Preferential and Plurality Voting." *Electoral Studies* 42: 157–163.

Drutman, Lee. 2015. *The Business of America Is Lobbying: How Corporations Became Politicized and Politics Became More Corporate*. New York: Oxford University Press.

Ebbert, Stephanie. 2022. "Cambodian Rise in Lowell Politics Shadowed by Dark History in Homeland." Boston Globe, February 6.

Einstein, Katherine Levine, and Vladimir Kogan. 2016. "Pushing the City Limits: Policy Responsiveness in Municipal Government." *Urban Affairs Review* 52 (1): 3–32.

Einstein, Katherine Levine, and David M. Glick. 2018. "Cities in American Federalism: Evidence on State–Local Government Conflict from a Survey of Mayors." *Publius: The Journal of Federalism* 48 (3): 504–553.

Feiock, Richard C. 2009. "Metropolitan Governance and Institutional Collective Action." *Urban Affairs Review* 44 (3): 356–377.

Fleischmann, Arnold, and Lana Stein. 1998. "Campaign Contributions in Local Elections." *Political Research Quarterly* 51 (3): 673–689.

Fouirnaies, Alexander, and Andrew B. Hall. 2014. "The Financial Incumbency Advantage: Causes and Consequences." *Journal of Politics* 76 (3): 711–724.

Fraga, Bernard. 2018. *The Turnout Gap: Race, Ethnicity, and Political Inequality in a Diversifying America.* New York: Cambridge University Press.

Francia, Peter L., John C. Green, Paul S. Herrnson, Lynda W. Powell, and Clyde Wilcox. 2003. *The Financiers of Congressional Elections: Investors, Ideologues, and Intimates.* New York: Columbia University Press.

Gaudette, Jennifer, and Justin de Benedictis-Kessner. 2024. "Local Money: Evaluating the Effects of Municipal Campaign Contributions on Housing Policy Outcomes." *Working Paper,* June 20. https://scholar.harvard.edu/sites/scholar.harvard.edu/files/jdbk/files/local_money.pdf.

Gaudette, Jennifer. 2025. "Polarization in Police Union Politics." *American Journal of Political Science* 69 (3): 961–980.

Gierzynski, Anthony. 2007. "Albuquerque Election Financing: An Analysis." Unpublished MS, University of Vermont.

Gilens, Martin. 2012. *Affluence and Influence.* Princeton, NJ: Princeton University Press.

Grumbach, Jake M., and Alexander Sahn. 2020. "Race and Representation in Campaign Finance." *American Political Science Review* 114 (1): 206–221.

Hajnal, Zoltan L., and Jessica Trounstine. 2005. "Where Turnout Matters: The Consequences of Uneven Turnout in City Politics." *Journal of Politics* 67 (2): 515–535.

Hajnal, Zoltan L. 2009. *America's Uneven Democracy: Race, Turnout, and Representation in City Politics.* New York: Cambridge University Press.

Hajnal, Zoltan L., Vladimir Kogan, and G. Agostin Markarian. 2022. "Who Votes: City Election Timing and Voter Composition." *American Political Science Review* 116 (1): 374–383.

Hartney, Michael T., and Sam D. Hayes. 2021. "Off-Cycle and Out of Sync: How Election Timing Influences Political Representation." *State Politics and Policy Quarterly* 21 (4): 335–354.

Hartney, Michael T. 2022. "Teachers' Unions and School Board Elections: A Reassessment." *Interest Groups & Advocacy* 11 (2): 237–262. https://doi.org/10.1057/s41309-022-00152-5.

Heaney, Michael T., Seth E. Masket, Joanne M. Miller, and Dara Z. Strolovitch. 2012. "Polarized Networks: The Organizational

Affiliations of National Party Convention Delegates." *American Behavioral Scientist* 56 (12): 1654–1676.
Heerwig, Jennifer A. 2016. "Donations and Dependence: Individual Contributor Strategies in House Elections." *Social Science Research* 60 (1): 181–198.
Heerwig, Jennifer A., and Brian J. McCabe. 2019. "High-Dollar Donors and Donor-Rich Neighborhoods: Representational Distortion in Financing Municipal Elections in Seattle." *Urban Affairs Review* 55(4): 1070–1099.
Hennessy, Carl Lynn. 2013. "Money and Influence in the Chicago City Council." *The Forum* 11 (3): 481–497.
Hertel-Fernandez, Alexander. 2018. *Politics at Work*. New York: Oxford University Press.
Hogan, Sean, and Dick Simpson. 2001. "Campaign Contributions and Mayoral/Aldermanic Relationships." *Urban Affairs Review* 37 (1): 85–95.
Holman, Craig. 2021. "Small Donors, Fair Elections: The Changing Nature of Financing D.C. Elections." Paper presented at the Annual Meeting of the American Political Science Association, Seattle, WA.
Homann, Jacqueline. 2016. "Get to Know America's Mid-Sized Cities." Metro Ideas Project, February 10. metroideas.org/blog/get-to-know-americas-midsize-cities/.
Hopkins, Daniel J. 2018. *The Increasingly United States: How and Why American Political Behavior Nationalized*. Chicago: University of Chicago Press.
Hunter, Floyd. 1953. *Community Power Structure: A Study of Decision Makers*. Chapel Hill: University of North Carolina Press.
Imbroscio, David L. 1997. *Reconstructing City Politics: Alternative Economic Development and Urban Regimes*. Thousand Oaks, CA: SAGE Publications.
Jacobson, Gary C. 1978. "The Effects of Campaign Spending in Congressional Elections." *American Political Science Review* 72 (2): 469–491.
Jacobson, Gary C. 1980. *Money in Congressional Elections*. New Haven, CT: Yale University Press.
Jensen, Jennifer M. and Thad Beyle. 2003. "Of Footnotes, Missing Data, and Lessons for 50-State Data Collection: The Gubernatorial Campaign Finance Project, 1977–2001." *State Politics and Policy Quarterly* 3 (2): 203–214.
Johnson, Bertram. 2010. "Individual Contributions: A Fundraising Advantage for the Ideologically Extreme?" *American Politics Research* 38 (5): 890–908.

Kaufmann, Karen M. 2004. *The Urban Voter*. Ann Arbor: University of Michigan Press.

Kim, Seo-young Silvia, and Bernard Fraga. 2022. "When Do Voter Files Accurately Measure Turnout? How Transitory Voter File Snapshots Impact Research and Representation." APSA Preprints. https://doi.org/10.33774/apsa-2022-qr0gd.

Kitchens, Karin E., and Michele L. Swers. 2016. "Why Aren't There More Republican Women in Congress? Gender, Partisanship, and Fundraising Support in the 2010 and 2012 Elections." *Politics & Gender* 12 (4): 1–29.

Kraus, Jeffrey. 2011. "Campaign Finance Reform Reconsidered: New York City's Public Finance Program at Twenty." In *Public Financing in American Elections*, edited by Costas Panagopoulos, 147–175. Philadelphia, PA: Temple University Press.

Krebs, Timothy B. 1998. "The Determinants of Candidates' Vote Share and the Advantages of Incumbency in City Council Elections." *American Journal of Political Science* 42 (3): 921–935.

Krebs, Timothy B., and John Pelissero. 2001. "Fund-Raising Coalitions in Mayoral Campaigns." *Urban Affairs Review* 37 (1): 67–84.

Krebs, Timothy B. 2004. "Explaining Corporate and Labor Contributions in Urban Elections." Paper presented at the Annual Meeting of the Midwest Political Science Association, Chicago, IL.

Kushner, Joseph, David Siegel, and Hannah Stanwick. 1997. "Ontario Municipal Elections: Voting Trends and Determinants of Electoral Success in a Canadian Province." *Canadian Journal of Political Science* 30 (3): 539–553.

La Raja, Raymond J., and Brian F. Schaffner. 2015. *Campaign Finance and Political Polarization: When Purists Prevail*. Ann Arbor: University of Michigan Press.

Lieske, Joel. 1989. "The Political Dynamics of Urban Voting Behavior." *American Journal of Political Science* 33 (1): 150–174.

Lowell Sun. 2013. "One Last Look at Election's Winners." Lowell Sun, November 10.

MacManus, Susan A., and Charles S. Bullock. 2003. "The Form, Structure, and Composition of America's Municipalities in the New Millennium." In *The Municipal Yearbook 2003*. Washington, DC: International City/County Management Association. www.lowellsun.com/2013/11/10/one-last-look-at-elections-winners/.

Magleby, David B., Jay Goodliffe, and Joseph A. Olson. 2018. *Who Donates in Campaigns?* New York: Cambridge University Press.

Makse, Todd, Scott Minkoff, and Anand Sokhey. 2019. *Politics on Display: Yard Signs and the Politicization of Social Spaces*. New York: Oxford University Press.

Malbin, Michael J. 2003. "Thinking about Reform." In *Life after Reform: When the Bipartisan Campaign Reform Act Meets Politics*, edited by Michael J. Malbin, 3–20. Lanham, MD: Rowman and Littlefield.

Malbin, Michael J., Peter W. Brusoe, and Brendan Glavin. 2012. "Small Donors, Big Democracy: New York City's Matching Funds as a Model for the Nation and States." *Election Law Journal* 11 (1): 3–20.

Malbin, Michael J., and Michael Parrott. 2017. "Small Donor Empowerment Depends on the Details: Comparing Matching Fund Programs in New York and Los Angeles." *The Forum* 15 (2): 219–250.

Martin, Danielle J., Brian E. Adams, and Edward L. Lascher. 2024. "Tribal Politics or Discerning Voters? Party and Policy in Local Elections." *Urban Affairs Review* 60 (6): 1871–1897.

Masket, Seth, and Boris Shor. 2015. "Polarization without Parties: Term Limits and Legislative Partisanship in Nebraska's Unicameral Legislature." *State Politics & Policy Quarterly* 15 (1): 67–90.

McCabe, Brian J., and Jennifer A. Heerwig. 2019. "Diversifying the Donor Pool: Did Seattle's Democracy Voucher Program Help Reshape Participation in Municipal Campaign Finance?" *Election Law Journal* 18 (4): 323–341.

McNamara, Neal. 2023. "Who's Funding New Worcester Super PAC? Donors from Business, Political Worlds." Patch.com, October 23. patch.com/massachusetts/worcester/progress-worcester-super-pac-donor-list-public-state-filing.

McNamara, Neal. 2024. "Worcester Councilors may Sideswipe Mill Street Design with New Orders." *Patch.com*, May 23. patch.com/massachusetts/worcester/mill-street-subject-multiple-worcester-city-council-orders.

Mills, Robert. 2019. "Attack Ads Roil Last Days of City Council Campaign." Lowell Sun, November 3. www.lowellsun.com/2019/11/03/attack-ads-roil-last-days-of-city-council-campaign/.

Mossberger, Karen, and Gerry Stoker. 2001. "The Evolution of Urban Regime Theory: The Challenge of Conceptualization." *Urban Affairs Review* 36 (6): 810–835.

Murphy, Matt. 2019. "Super PAC with Ties to Baker Spends Deep." Worcester Telegram, November 2. www.telegram.com/story/news/local/east-valley/2019/11/02/leominster-developer-leads-super-pac-with-ties-to-baker/2384986007/.

Newman, Mark E. J., and Michelle Girvan. 2004. "Finding and Evaluating Community Structure in Networks." *Physical Review* 69 (2): 026113.

Oliver, J. Eric, Shang E. Ha, and Zachary Callan. 2012. *Local Elections and the Politics of Small-Scale Democracy*. Princeton, NJ: Princeton University Press.

Open Secrets. 2023. "Financial Activity for All House Candidates, 2021–2022." OpenSecrets, April 18. www.opensecrets.org/elections-overview?cycle=2022.

Open Secrets. 2023. "PAC Dollars to Incumbents, Challengers, and Open Seat Candidates." OpenSecrets, April 18. www.opensecrets.org/elections-overview/pacs-stick-with-incumbents.

Peterson, Paul E. 1981. *City Limits*. Chicago: University of Chicago Press.

Powell, Lynda W. 2012. *The Influence of Campaign Contributions in State Legislatures*. Ann Arbor: University of Michigan Press.

Raetz, Hayley. 2021. "Housing Characteristics of Small and Mid-Sized Cities." New York: The Furman Center, January 27. furmancenter.org/thestoop/entry/housing-characteristics-of-small-and-mid-sized-cities.

Rolfe, Meredith. 2014. "Social Networks and Agent-based Modelling." In *Analytical Sociology*, edited by Gianluco Manzo, 233–260. New York: John Wiley & Sons.

Rosengren, Eric S. 2012. "Strengthening New England's Smaller Cities." Federal Reserve Bank of Boston, September 24. www.bostonfed.org/news-and-events/speeches/strengthening-new-englands-smaller-cities.aspx#importance.

Santucci, Jack. 2022. *More Parties or No Parties?* New York: Oxford University Press.

Schaffner, Brian F., Matthew Streb, and Gerald Wright. 2001. "Teams without Uniforms: The Nonpartisan Ballot in State and Local Elections," *Political Research Quarterly* 54 (1): 7–30.

Schaffner, Brian F., Jesse H. Rhodes, and Raymond J. La Raja. 2020. *Hometown Inequality: Race, Class, and Representation in American Local Politics*. New York: Cambridge University Press.

Schiff, Kaylyn. 2022. "Who Participates in Local Government? Evidence from Meeting Minutes." *American Political Science Review* 116 (1): 222–230.

Schlozman, Kay Lehman, Sidney Verba, and Henry L. Brady. 2012. *The Unheavenly Chorus*. Princeton, NJ: Princeton University Press.

Schmitt, Mark. 2021. "Democracy Reforms go Better Together." New America, July 15. Online, www.newamerica.org/political-reform/briefs/democracy-reforms-go-better-together/.

Snowden, Jonah. 2023. "Springfield City Council Asks Mayor to Pause Trash Fees in 2023." Springfield Republican, January 10. www.masslive.com/springfield/2023/01/springfield-city-council-asks-mayor-to-pause-trash-fees-in-2023.html.

Stone, Clarence N. 1989. *Regime Politics*. Lawrence: University Press of Kansas.

Stone, Clarence N. 2005. "Looking Back to Look Forward: Reflections on Urban Regime Analysis." *Urban Affairs Review* 40 (3): 309–341.

Straus, Graham. 2025. "The Economic Background of City Councilmembers." *Urban Affairs Review*. https://doi.org/10.1177/10780874251315148.

Svara, James H. 1990. *Official Leadership in the City: Patterns of Conflict and Cooperation*. New York: Oxford University Press.

Tausanovitch, Chris, and Christopher Warshaw. 2014. "Representation in Municipal Government." *American Political Science Review* 108 (3): 605–641.

Tausanovitch, Chris, and Christopher Warshaw. 2021. "Estimating Candidates' Political Orientation in a Polarized Congress." *Political Analysis* 29 (3): 360–378.

Thomsen, Danielle M., and Michele L. Swers. 2017. "Which Women Can Run? Gender, Partisanship, and Candidate Donor Networks." *Political Research Quarterly* 70 (2): 449–463.

Trounstine, Jessica. 2008. *Political Monopolies in American Cities*. Chicago: University of Chicago Press.

Trounstine, Jessica. 2010. "Representation and Accountability in Cities." *Annual Review of Political Science* 13 (1): 407–423.

Trounstine, Jessica. 2018. *Segregation by Design: Local Politics and Inequality in American Cities*. New York: Cambridge University Press.

Trounstine, Jessica, and Melody E. Valdini. 2008. "The Context Matters: The Effects of Single-Member versus At-Large Districts on City Council Diversity." *American Journal of Political Science* 52 (3): 554–569. https://doi.org/0.1111/j.1540-5907.2008.00329.x.

Yorgason, Chenoa. 2024. "Campaign Finance Vouchers Do Not Expand the Diversity of Donors: Evidence from Seattle." *American Political Science Review*, March 22, 1–9. https://doi.org/10.1017/S0003055424000170.

Acknowledgments

This project originated in 2007 as a way to help Clark University undergraduates understand how campaign finance worked in the city where they live. A number of Worcester city council members have generously given these students firsthand accounts of how money is raised in local elections. In particular, Tracy O'Connell Novick and Nicole Apostola offered feedback and encouragement about gathering data on Worcester elections and campaign finance. Jim Gomes, former director of the William Mosakowski Institute for Public Enterprise at Clark University, provided seed funding for some of the early research related to this project, as part of a project on midsize American cities led by the Federal Reserve Bank of Boston.

Once this developed into a broader study of municipal campaign finance, our colleagues Wouter van Erve, Zachary Albert, and Caroline Tolbert were invaluable in helping us understand how to use Catalist data. Many student research assistants, including Sarah Kersting-Mumm, Matt Lee, Shanay Massimi, Anna Walker, and Ruthie Brian (Clark University); Cole Bates (Texas Woman's University); Mandy Feuerman (Brandeis University), Alan Svendsen (Bowdoin College); and Samantha Weiss and Matt Peranowski (University of Massachusetts, Amherst) helped gather data. David Glick, Michael McGregor, and Peter Ubertaccio offered feedback at conference presentations of earlier versions of this material. Richard Howe reviewed the Lowell information for accuracy, and Robert Winters reviewed the Cambridge material.

We received financial support for the Catalist analysis in this project from Unite America, as part of a larger inquiry into the relationship between ranked-choice voting and campaign finance; and from the Task Force on American Electoral Reform, chaired by Larry Diamond, Edward Foley, and Richard Pildes, and funded by Arnold Ventures and the Skoll Foundation. We thank our colleagues on this task force, and we thank Beth Hladick and Tyler Fisher at Unite America for their support.

American Politics

Frances E. Lee
Princeton University

Frances E. Lee is Professor of Politics at the Woodrow Wilson School of Princeton University. She is author of *Insecure Majorities: Congress and the Perpetual Campaign* (2016), *Beyond Ideology: Politics, Principles and Partisanship in the U.S. Senate* (2009), and coauthor of *Sizing Up the Senate: The Unequal Consequences of Equal Representation* (1999).

Advisory Board

Larry M. Bartels, *Vanderbilt University*
Marc Hetherington, *University of North Carolina at Chapel Hill*
Geoffrey C. Layman, *University of Notre Dame*
Suzanne Mettler, *Cornell University*
Hans Noel, *Georgetown University*
Eric Schickler, *University of California, Berkeley*
John Sides, *George Washington University*
Laura Stoker, *University of California, Berkeley*

About the Series

The Cambridge Elements Series in *American Politics* publishes authoritative contributions on American politics. Emphasizing works that address big, topical questions within the American political landscape, the series is open to all branches of the subfield and actively welcomes works that bridge subject domains. It publishes both original new research on topics likely to be of interest to a broad audience and state-of-the-art synthesis and reconsideration pieces that address salient questions and incorporate new data and cases to inform arguments.

Cambridge Elements

American Politics

Elements in the Series

Why Bad Policies Spread (and Good Ones Don't)
Charles R. Shipan and Craig Volden

The Partisan Next Door: Stereotypes of Party Supporters and Consequences for Polarization in America
Ethan C. Busby, Adam J. Howat, Jacob E. Rothschild and Richard M. Shafranek

The Dynamics of Public Opinion
Mary Layton Atkinson, K. Elizabeth Coggins, James A. Stimson and Frank R. Baumgartner

The Origins and Consequences of Congressional Party Election Agendas
Scott R. Meinke

The Full Armor of God: The Mobilization of Christian Nationalism in American Politics
Paul A. Djupe, Andrew R. Lewis and Anand E. Sokhey

The Dimensions and Implications of the Public's Reactions to the January 6, 2021, Invasion of the U.S. Capitol
Gary C. Jacobson

Cooperating Factions: A Network Analysis of Party Divisions in U.S. Presidential Nominations
Rachel M. Blum, Hans C. Noel

The Haves and Have-Nots in Supreme Court Representation and Participation, 2016 to 2021
Kirsten Widner and Anna Gunderson

The Political Dynamics of Partisan Polarization
Eric R. Schmidt, Edward G. Carmines and Paul M. Sniderman

Congressional Expectations of Presidential Self-Restraint
Jack B. Greenberg and John A. Dearborn

Shifting Allegiances: The Election of Latino Republicans to Congress and State Legislatures
Robert D. Alvarez and Jason P. Casellas

Money, Partisanship and Power in Local Politics
Robert G. Boatright, Lane Cuthbert, Adam Eichen, Raymond J. La Raja, and Meredith Rolfe

A full series listing is available at: www.cambridge.org/EAMP

For EU product safety concerns, contact us at Calle de José Abascal, 56–1°, 28003 Madrid, Spain or eugpsr@cambridge.org.

www.ingramcontent.com/pod-product-compliance
Lightning Source LLC
LaVergne TN
LVHW011847060526
838200LV00054B/4211